Monsieur
Emile de Laveleye
with H W Freeland's
Kind Regards.

AN

HISTORICAL ACCOUNT

OF

TWO NOTABLE

CORRUPTIONS OF SCRIPTURE:

IN A LETTER TO A FRIEND.

BY

SIR ISAAC NEWTON.

PUBLISHED ENTIRE FROM A MS. IN THE AUTHOR'S HAND-WRITING
IN THE POSSESSION OF THE REV. DR. EKENS,
DEAN OF CARLISLE.

*Exactly reprinted from Bishop Horsley's Edition of Sir Isaac Newton's
Works*, vol. v. 1785.

Watchmaker Publishing
1841.

ISBN 978-1-60386-422-0

BISHOP HORSLEY'S

ADVERTISEMENT.

A VERY imperfect copy of this Tract, wanting both the beginning and the end, and
erroneous in many places, was published at
London in the year 1754, under the title of
Two Letters from Sir Isaac Newton to Mr.
Le Clerc. But in the Author's MS. the
whole is one continued discourse; which, although it is conceived in the epistolary form,
is not addressed to any particular person.

AN

HISTORICAL ACCOUNT

OF

TWO NOTABLE CORRUPTIONS

OF SCRIPTURE.

IN A LETTER TO A FRIEND.

BY SIR ISAAC NEWTON.

SIR,

SINCE the discourses of some late writers have
raised in you a curiosity of knowing the truth of
that text of Scripture concerning the testimony
of the Three in Heaven, 1 John v. 7, I have here
sent you an account of what the reading has been
in all ages, and by what steps it has been changed,
so far as I can hitherto determine by records.
And I have done it the more freely, because to you,
who understand the many abuses which they of
the Roman church have put upon the world, it
will scarce be ungrateful to be convinced of one
more than is commonly believed. For although
the more learned and quick-sighted men, as
Luther, Erasmus, Bullinger, Grotius, and some

others, would not dissemble their knowledge, yet the generality are fond of the place for its making against heresy. But whilst we exclaim against the pious frauds of the Roman church, and make it a part of our religion to detect and renounce all things of that kind, we must acknowledge it a greater crime in us to favour such practices, than in the Papists we so much blame on that account: for they act according to their religion, but we contrary to ours. In the Eastern nations, and for a long time in the Western, the faith subsisted without this text; and it is rather a danger to religion, than an advantage, to make it now lean upon a bruised reed. There cannot be better service done to the truth, than to purge it of things spurious: and therefore knowing your prudence, and calmness of temper, I am confident I shall not offend you by telling you my mind plainly; especially since it is no article of faith, no point of discipline, nothing but a criticism concerning a text of Scripture which I am going to write about.

II. The history of the corruption, in short, is this. First, some of the Latines interpreted the Spirit, Water, and Blood, of the Father, Son, and Holy Ghost, to prove them one. Then Jerome, for the same end, inserted the Trinity in express words into his version. Out of him the Africans began to allege it against the Vandals, about sixty-four years after his death. Afterwards the Latines noted his variations in the margins of their books; and thence it began at length to creep into the text in transcribing, and that chiefly in the twelfth and following centuries, when disputing was revived by the schoolmen. And when printing came up, it crept out of the Latine into the printed Greek, against the authority of all the Greek manuscripts and ancient versions; and from the Venetian presses it went soon after into Greece. Now the truth of this history will appear by considering the arguments on both sides.

III. The arguments alleged for the testimony of the Three in Heaven, are the authorities of Cyprian, Athanasius, and Jerome, and of many Greek manuscripts, and almost all the Latine ones.

IV. Cyprian's words[1] run thus—"the Lord saith, 'I and the Father am one.' And again of the Father, Son, and Holy Ghost it is written, 'And these Three are One.'" The Socinians here deal too injuriously with Cyprian, while they would have this place corrupted: for Cyprian in another place repeats almost the same thing[2]. "If," saith he, [" one baptized among heretics] be made the temple of God, tell me, I pray, of

---

[1] "Dicit Dominus, Ego et pater unum sumus; et iterum de patre et filio et spiritu sancto scriptum est, Et tres unum sunt."—*Cypr. de Unit. Eccles.*

[2] "Si templum Dei factus est, quæso cujus Dei? Si spiritus sancti, cum tres unum sint, quomodo spiritus sanctus placatus ei esse potest, qui aut patris aut filii inimicus est?"—*Cypr. Epist.* 73, *ad Jubaianum.*

what God ? If of the Holy Ghost, since these
Three are One, how can the Holy Ghost be reconciled to him who is the enemy of either the
Father or the Son ?" These places of Cyprian
being, in my opinion, genuine, seem so apposite
to prove the testimony of the Three in Heaven,
that I should never have suspected a mistake in
it, could I but have reconciled it with the ignorance
I meet with of this reading in the next age,
amongst the Latines of both Africa and Europe,
as well as among the Greeks. For had it been
in Cyprian's Bible, the Latines of the next age,
when all the world was engaged in disputing about
the Trinity, and all arguments that could be
thought of were diligently sought out, and daily
brought upon the stage, could never have been
ignorant of a text, which in our age, now the
dispute is over, is chiefly insisted upon. In re-
conciling this difficulty, I consider, therefore, that
the only words of the text quoted by Cyprian in
both places are, " And these Three are One:"
which words may belong to the eighth verse as
well as to the seventh. For Eucherius[1] bishop

---

[1] Eucherius reads the text thus : "Tria sunt quæ testimonium perhibent ; aqua, sanguis, et spiritus." And then adds
this interpretation, " Plures hìc ipsam, interpretatione mystica,
intelligunt Trinitatem ; eò quod perfecta ipsa perhibeat testimonium Christo : aqua, patrem indicans ; quia ipse de se
dicit, me dereliquerunt fontem aquæ vivæ : sanguine, Christum
demonstrans, utique per passionis cruorem : spiritu verò
sanctum spiritum manifestans."—*Eucher. de Quæst. N. Test.*

of Lion in France, and contemporary to St. Austin,
reading the text without the seventh verse, tells
us, that many then understood the Spirit, the
Water, and the Blood, to signify the Trinity.
And St. Austin[1] is one of those many; as you
may see in his third book against Maximus, where
he tells us, that "the Spirit is the Father, for
God is a Spirit: the Water the Holy Ghost, for
he is the Water which Christ gives to them that
thirst: and the Blood the Son, for the Word was
made flesh."   Now if it was the opinion of many
in the Western churches of those times, that the
Spirit, the Water, and the Blood, signified the
Father, the Son, and the Holy Ghost; it is plain
that the testimony of Three in Heaven, in express

[1] " Sanè falli te nolo in epistolâ Joannis Apostoli, ubi ait,
' tres sunt testes, spiritus, aqua, et sanguis, et tres unum sunt ;'
ne fortè dicas, spiritum et aquam et sanguinem diversas esse
substantias, et tamen dictam [*dictum*] esse, tres unum sunt.
Propter hoc admonui te, ne fallaris : hæc enim sunt, in quibus non quid sint, sed quid ostendant, semper attenditur.   Si
verò ea, quæ his significata sunt, velimus inquirere ; non ab-
surdè occurrit ipsa Trinitas, quæ unus, solus, summus est
Deus, pater et filius et spiritus sanctus ; de quibus verissimè
dici potuit, tres sunt testes, et tres unum sunt : ut nomine
spiritûs significatum accipiamus Deum patrem, (de Deo ipso
quippe adorando loquebatur Dominus, ubi ait, 'spiritus est
Deus ;') nomine autem sanguinis, filium ; quia verbum caro
factum est : nomine autem aquæ, spiritum sanctum.   Cùm
enim de aquâ loqueretur Jesus, quam daturus erat sitientibus,
ait evangelista ; ' Hoc autem dicit de spiritu, quem accepturi
erant credentes in eum.' "—*D. Augustin. cont. Maximum.*
lib. iii. cap. xxii.

words, was not yet crept into their books : and even without this testimony, it was obvious for Cyprian, or any man else of that opinion, to say of the Father, and Son, and Holy Ghost, " it is written, ' And these Three are One.' " And that this was Cyprian's meaning, Facundus[1], an African bishop in the sixth century, is my author ; for he tells us expressly that Cyprian, in the above-mentioned place, understood it so, interpreting the Water, Spirit, and Blood, to be the

---

[1] Facundus, in the beginning of his book to the Emperor Justinian, *Pro Defensione trium Capitulorum Consilii Chalcedonensis,* first recites the text after the manner of Cyprian, but more distinctly in these words : " Nam Joannes apostolus, in epistolâ suâ, de patre et filio et spiritu sancto sic dicit, ' Tres sunt, qui testimonium dant in terrâ, spiritus, aqua, et sanguis ; et hi tres unum sunt ;' in spiritu significans patrem, &c. Joan. iv. 21. In aquâ spiritum sanctum, Joan. vii. 37 ; in sanguine verò filium." And a little after he thus confirms this interpretation by Cyprian's authority, saying, " Aut si forsan ipsi, qui de verbo contendunt, in eo quod dixit, ' Tres sunt qui testificantur in terrâ, spiritus, aqua, et sanguis, et hi tres unum sunt,' Trinitatem nolunt intelligi ; secundum ipsa verba quæ posuit, pro apostolo Joanne respondeant. Numquid hi tres, qui in terrâ testificari, et qui unum esse dicuntur, possunt spiritus et aquæ et sanguines dici ? Quod tamen Joannis apostoli testimonium B. Cyprianus Carthaginensis, antistes et martyr, in epistolâ sive libro quem de Trinitate, immò de Unitate Ecclesiæ scripsit, de patre, filio, et spiritu sancto dictum intelligit : ait enim, ' dicit dominus, ego et pater unum sumus ; et iterum de patre, filio, et spiritu sancto scriptum est, et hi tres unum sunt.' "—*Facund. lib.* i. *p.* 16 ; *ex edit. Sirmondi, Parisiis,* 1629,

Father, Son, and Holy Ghost; and thence affirming that John said of the Father, Son, and Holy Ghost, "these Three are One." This at least may be gathered from this passage of Facundus, that some in those early ages interpreted Cyprian after this manner. Nor do I understand how any of those many who took the Spirit, Water, and Blood, for a type of the Trinity; or any man else, who was ignorant of the testimony of the Three in Heaven, as the churches in the times of the Arian controversy generally were, could understand him otherwise. And even Cyprian's own words do plainly make for the interpretation. For he does not say, "the Father, the Word, and the Holy Ghost," as it is now in the seventh verse; but "the Father, and Son, and Holy Ghost," as it is in baptism; the place from which they tried * at first to derive the Trinity. If it be pretended, that the words cited by Cyprian are taken out of the seventh verse, rather than out of the eighth, because he reads not, "*Hi Tres in Unum sunt,*" but "*Hi Tres Unum sunt;*" I answer, that the Latines generally read, "*Hi Tres Unum sunt,*" as well in the eighth verse, as in the seventh; as you may see in the newly cited places of St. Austin and Facundus, and those of Ambrose, Pope Leo, Beda, and Cassiodorus, which follow,

* *The insinuation contained in this expression, that the Trinity is not to be derived from the words prescribed for the baptismal form, is very extraordinary to come from a writer who was no Socinian.*—Bp. Horsley.

and in the present vulgar Latine. So then the testimony of Cyprian respects the eighth, or at least is as applicable to that verse as to the seventh, and therefore is of no force for proving the truth of the seventh : but on the contrary, for disproving it we have here the testimony of Facundus, St. Austin, Eucherius, and those many others whom Eucherius mentions. For if those of that age had met with it in their books, they would never have understood the Spirit, the Water, and the Blood, to be the Three Persons of the Trinity, in order to prove them One God.

V. These passages in Cyprian may receive further light by a like passage in Tertullian, from whence Cyprian seems to have borrowed them ; for it is well known that Cyprian was a great admirer of Tertullian's writings, and read them frequently, calling Tertullian his master. The passage is this [1]: "The connection of the Father in the Son, and of the Son in the Paraclete, makes three coherent ones from one another, which Three are One (one thing, not one person,) as it is said, 'I and the Father are One ;' denoting the Unity of substance, not the singularity of number." Here, you see, Tertullian says not, "the Father, Word, and Holy Ghost," as the text now has it,

[1] "Connexus patris in filio, et filii in paracleto, tres efficit cohærentes, alterum ex altero, 'qui Tres Unum sunt,' (non Unus) quomodo dictum est, 'Ego et Pater Unum sumus ;' ad substantiæ unitatem, non ad numeri singularitatem."—*Tertullian. advers. Prax.* cap. 25.

but "the Father, Son, and Paraclete;" nor cites anything more of the text than these words, "which Three are One." Though this treatise against St. Praxeas be wholly spent in discoursing about the Trinity, and all texts of Scripture are cited to prove it, and this text of St. John, as we now read it, would have been one of the most obvious and apposite to have been cited at large, yet Tertullian could find no more obvious words in it for his purpose than "these Three are One." These, therefore, he interprets of the Trinity, and inforces the interpretation by that other text, "I and the Father are One;" as if the phrase was of the same importance in both places.

VI. So then this interpretation seems to have been invented by the Montanists for giving countenance to their Trinity. For Tertullian was a Montanist when he wrote this; and it is most likely that so corrupt and forced an interpretation had its rise among a sect of men accustomed to make bold with the Scriptures. Cyprian being used to it in his master's writings, it seems from thence to have dropt into his: for this may be gathered from the likeness between their citations. And by the disciples of these two great men, it seems to have been propagated among those many Latins, who (as Eucherius tells us) received it in the next age, understanding the Trinity by the "Spirit, Water, and Blood." For how, without the countenance of some such authority, an interpretation so corrupt and strained should come

to be received in that age so generally, I do not
understand.

VII. And what is said of the testimony of Tertullian and Cyprian, may be much more said
of that in the feigned disputation of Athanasius
with Arius at Nice. For there the words cited
are only "και οἱ τρεις το ἑν εισιν," "and these
Three are One ;" and they are taken out of the
seventh verse, without naming the persons of the
Trinity before them. For the Greeks interpreted
"the Spirit, Water, and Blood," of the Trinity,
as well as the Latins ; as is manifest from the annotations they made on this text in the margin of
some of their manuscripts. For Father Simon[1]
informs us that in one of the manuscripts in the
library of the king of France, marked numb.
2247, over against these words, "ὁτι τρεις εισιν
οἱ μαρτυρουντες εν τῃ γῃ[2], το πνευμα και το ὑδωρ
και το αἱμα," "for there are Three that bear record [in earth,] the Spirit, the Water, and the
Blood ;" there is this remark, "τουτεστι, το
πνευμα το ἁγιον, και ὁ πατηρ, και αὑτος ἑαυτου,"
"that is, the Holy Ghost, and the Father, and
He of Himself." And in the same copy over
against these words, "και οἱ τρεις εις το ἑν εισι,"
"and these Three are One ;" this note is added,
"τουτεστι, μια θεοτης, εἱς θεος," that is, "One
Deity, One God." This manuscript is about 500
years old.

---

[1] Critical History of the New Testament : cap. 18.
[2] Suspicor verba *ευ τῃ γῃ* non extare in MS.

VIII. Also in the margin of one of the manuscripts in Monsieur Colbert's library, numb. 871,
Father Simon tells us there is a like remark. For
besides these words, " εἰς θεος, μια θεοτης, "
" One God, One Godhead;" there are added,
" μαρτυρια του θεου του πατρος και του ἁγιου
πνευματος." "The testimony of God, the Father,
and of the Holy Ghost." These marginal notes
sufficiently show how the Greeks used to apply
this text to the Trinity; and by consequence how
the author of that disputation is to be understood.
But I should tell you also, that that disputation
was not writ by Athanasius, but by a later author,
and therefore, as a spurious piece, uses not to be
much insisted upon.

IX. Now this mystical application of "the
Spirit, Water, and Blood," to signify the Trinity,
seems to me to have given occasion to somebody,
either fraudulently to insert the testimony of "the
Three in Heaven" in express words into the text,
for proving the Trinity; or else to note it in the
margin of his book, by way of interpretation;
whence it might afterwards creep into the text in
transcribing. And the first upon record that inserted it, is Jerome; if the preface[1] to the canoni-

---

[1] The whole preface runs thus : " Incipit prologus in epistolas canonicas. Non ita est ordo apud Græcos, qui integrè
sapiunt, fidemque rectam sectantur, epistolarum septem, quæ
canonicæ nuncupantur, sicut in Latinis codicibus invenitur :
ut quia Petrus est primus in ordine apostolorum, primæ sint
etiam ejus epistolæ in ordine ceterarum. Sed sicut evange-

cal epistles, which goes under his name, be his.
For whilst he composed not a new translation of
the New Testament, but only corrected the ancient vulgar Latin (as learned men think), and
among his emendations (written perhaps at first
in the margin of his book) he inserted this testimony; he complains in the said preface, how he
was thereupon accused* by some of the Latins
for falsifying Scripture; and makes answer, that

listas dudum ad veritatis lineam correximus, ita has proprio
ordini, Deo juvante, reddidimus. Est enim una earum prima
Jacobi, duæ Petri, tres Johannis, et Judæ una. Quæ si sicut
ab eis digestæ sunt, ita quoque ab interpretibus fideliter in
Latinum verterentur eloquium, nec ambiguitatem legentibus
facerent, nec sermonum sese varietates impugnarent, illo præ-
cipuè loco ubi de Unitate Trinitatis in primâ Johannis epistolâ,
positum legimus, &c. In quâ etiam ab infidelibus translato-
ribus, multum erratum esse à fidei veritate comperimus, trium
tantummodo vocabula, hoc est, Aquæ, Sanguinis, et Spiritûs,
in ipsâ suâ editione ponentibus : et Patris, Verbique, ac Spiritûs testimonium omittentibus ; in quo maximè et fides ca-
tholica roboratur, et patris, ac filii, et spiritûs una divinitatis
substantia comprobatur. In cæteris verò epistolis, quantum
à nostrâ aliorum distet editio, lectoris judicio derelinquo. Sed
tu, virgo Christi Eustochium, dum à me impensiùs scripturæ
veritatem inquiris, meam quodammodo senectutem invidorum
dentibus corrodendam exponis, qui me falsarium, corruptorem-
que sanctarum pronunciant scripturarum. Sed ego, in tali
opere, nec æmulorum meorum invidiam pertimesco, nec Sanc-
tæ Scripturæ veritatem poscentibus denegabo.''

* *Jerome complains not of any accusation raised upon what
he had done in this or any other particular text of Scripture.
He affirms, that this text was unfaithfully rendered in the
Latin Bibles, which were current in his time before his own*

former Latin translators had much erred from the faith, in putting only "the Spirit, Water, and Blood," in their edition, and omitting the testimony of "the Three in Heaven," whereby the Catholic faith is established. In his defence he seems to say, that he corrected the vulgar Latin translation by the original Greek; and this is the great testimony the text relies upon.

X. But whilst he confesses it was not in the Latin before, and accuses former translators of falsifying the Scriptures in omitting it, he satisfies us that it has crept into the Latin since his time, and so cuts off all the authority of the present vulgar Latin for justifying it. And whilst he was accused by his contemporaries of falsifying the Scriptures in inserting it, this accusation also confirms, that he altered the public reading. For had the reading been dubious before he made it so, no man would have charged him with falsification for following either part. Also whilst, upon this accusation, he recommends the alteration by its usefulness for establishing the Catholic faith, this renders it the more suspected; by discovering both the design of his making it, and the ground of his hoping for success. However, seeing he was thus accused by his contempora-

edition. That his edition, in this as well as in other passages, faithfully represented the original Greek; and he expresses an apprehension, that the number of his emendations, which the infidelity of former translators had rendered necessary, might furnish his enemies with a pretence for abuse.—Bp. Horsley.

ries, it gives us just reason to examine the business between him and his accusers. And so, he being called to the bar, we are not to lay stress upon his own testimony for himself, (for no man is a witness in his own cause,) but laying aside all prejudice, we ought, according to the ordinary rules of justice, to examine the business between him and his accusers by other witnesses.

XI. They that have been conversant in his writings, observe a strange liberty which he takes in asserting things. Many notable instances of this he has left us in composing those very fabulous lives of Paul and Hilarion, not to mention what he has written upon other occasions. Whence Erasmus said of him, that he was in affirming things, " frequently violent and impudent, and often contrary to himself[1]." But I accuse him not. It is possible that he might be sometimes imposed upon, or, through inadvertency, commit a mistake. Yet since his contemporaries accused him, it is but just that we should lay aside the prejudice of his great name, and hear the cause impartially between them.

XII. Now the witnesses between them are partly the ancient translators of the Scriptures into the various languages ; partly the writers of his own age, and of the ages next before and

---

[1] " Sæpe numero violentus, parumque pudens, sæpe varius, parumque sibi constans."—*Erasmi Annotation. in Johan.* v. 7.

Vide etiam quæ Erasmus contra Leum in hunc locum de Hieronymo fusiùs dixit.

after him; and partly the Scribes who have copied out the Greek manuscripts of the Scriptures in all ages. And all these are against him. For by the unanimous evidence of all these, it will appear that the testimony of "the Three in Heaven" was wanting in the Greek manuscripts, from whence Jerome, or whoever was the author of that preface to the canonical epistles, pretends to have borrowed it.

XIII. The ancient interpreters, which I cite as witnesses against him, are chiefly the authors of the ancient vulgar Latin, of the Syriac, and the Æthiopic versions. For as he tells us, that the Latins omitted the testimony of "the Three in Heaven" in their version before his time, so in the Syriac and Æthiopic versions, (both which, from bishop Walton's account of them, are much ancienter than Jerome's time, being the versions which the Oriental and Æthiopic nations received from the beginning, and generally used, as the Latins did the vulgar Latin,) that same testimony is wanting to this day; and the authors of these three most ancient, most famous, and most received versions, by omitting it, are concurrent witnesses, that they found it wanting in the original Greek manuscripts of their own times. It is wanting also in other ancient versions; as in the Egyptian Arabic, published in Walton's Polyglot; in the Armenian version[1], used, ever

[1] "Codex Armeniacus ante 400 annos exaratus, quem vidi apud Episcopum Ecclesiæ Armeniacæ, quæ Amstelodami col-

since Chrysostom's age, by the Armenian nations; and in the Illyrican[1] of Cyrillus, used in
Rascia, Bulgaria, Moldavia, Russia, Muscovy,
and other countries, which use the Sclavonic
tongue. In a copy of this version[1], printed at
Ostrobe (Ostrow) in Volhinia, in the year 1581,
I have seen it wanting; and one Camillus[2] relates the same thing out of ancient manuscripts
of this version seen by him. Father Simon notes
it wanting also in a certain version of the French
church, which, saith he, is at least 1000 years
old, and which was published by Father Mabillon,
a Benedictine monk. Nor do I know of any version wherein it is extant, except the modern vulgar Latin, and such modern versions, of the
Western nations, as have been influenced by it.
So then, by the unanimous consent of all the ancient and faithful interpreters which we have hitherto met with, (who doubtless made use of the
best manuscripts they could get,) the testimony

ligitur, locum illum non legit."—*Sandius Append. Interpret.
Paradox. in h. l.*

[1] The printed Sclavonic version runs thus: "Quia Tres
sunt qui testificantur, Spiritus, et Aqua, et Sanguis; et Tres
in Unum sunt. Si testimonium," &c.

[2] "Testimonium trium in Cœlo non est in antiquissimis
Illyricorum et Ruthenorum codicibus; quorum unum exemplar, à sexcentis ferè annis manuscriptum, jampridem apud
illustrissimum Gabrielem Chineum, terræ Bactricæ Dominum
vidi, et legi: alterum manibus nostris teritur, fide et anti-
quitate suâ nobile."—*Camillus de Antichristo,* lib. ii. cap. 2.
pag. 156.

of " the Three in Heaven" was not anciently in the Greek.

XIV. And that it was neither in the ancient versions nor in the Greek, but was wholly unknown to the first churches, is most certain by an argument hinted above; namely, that in all that vehement, universal, and lasting controversy about the Trinity in Jerome's time, and both before and long enough after it, this text of " the Three in Heaven" was never once thought of. It is now in everybody's mouth, and accounted the main text for the business, and would assuredly have been so too with them, had it been in their books. And yet it is not once to be met with in all the disputes, epistles, orations, and other writings of the Greeks and Latins (Alexander of Alexandria, Athanasius, the council of Sardica, Basil, Nazianzen, Nyssen, Epiphanius, Chrysostom, Cyril, Theodoret, Hilary, Ambrose, Austin, Victorinus Afer, Philastrius Brixiensis, Phæbedius Agennensis, Gregorius Bæticus, Faustinus Diaconus, Paschasius, Arnobius Junior, Cerealis and others,) in the times of those controversies; no, not in Jerome himself; if his version and preface to the canonical epistles be excepted. The writings of those times were very many, and copious; and there is no argument, or text of Scripture, which they do not urge again and again. That of St. John's gospel, " I and the Father am One," is everywhere inculcated, but this of " the Three in Heaven, and their being One," is nowhere to be met with, till at length, when the ignorant ages came on, it began by degrees to creep into the Latin copies out of Jerome's version. So far are they from citing the testimony of "the Three in Heaven," that, on the contrary, as often as they have occasion to mention the place, they omit it, and that too, as well after Jerome's age, as in and before it. For Hesychius[1] cites the place thus: "*Audi Johannem dicentem, Tria sunt qui testimonium præbent, et Tres Unum sunt, spiritus, et sanguis, et aqua.*" The words '*in terrâ*' he omits, which is never done, but in copies where "the Three in Heaven" is wanting. Cassiodorus, or whoever was the author of the Latin version of the discourse of Clemens Alexandrinus on these epistles of St. John, reads it thus: "*Quia tres sunt, qui testificantur, spiritus, et aqua, et sanguis; et hi Tres Unum sunt[2].*" Beda, in his commentary on the place, reads it thus: "*Et spiritus est qui testificatur, quoniam Christus est veritas. Quoniam Tres sunt, qui testimonium dant in terrâ, spiritus, aqua, et sanguis, et Tres Unum sunt. Si testimonium,*" &c. But here the words, in '*terrâ,*' so far as I can gather from his commentary on this text, have been inserted by some latter hand. The author of the first epistle, ascribed to Pope Eusebius, reads it, as Beda doth, omitting only the words, *in terrâ.* And if the authority of popes

---

[1] Hesych. in Levit. lib. ii. c. 8. post med.
[2] Cassiodor. in Bibl. S. Patr. edit. Paris. 1589.

be valuable, Pope Leo the Great, in his tenth epistle, thus cites the place : " *Et spiritus est qui testificatur, quoniam spiritus est veritas ; quia Tres sunt qui testimonium dant, spiritus, et aqua, et sanguis; et hi Tres Unum sunt.*" St. Ambrose, in the sixth chapter of his first book, *De Spiritu Sancto,* disputing for the unity of the Three Persons, says, " *Hi Tres Unum sunt, Johannes dixit, aqua, sanguis, et spiritus : Unum in mysterio, non in naturâ.*" This is all he could find of the text, while he was disputing about the Trinity, and therefore he proves the unity of the persons by the mystical unity of the Spirit, Water, and Blood : interpreting these of the Trinity with Cyprian and others. Yea, in the eleventh chapter of his third book, he fully recites the text thus : " *Per aquam et sanguinem venit Christus Jesus, non solùm in aquâ, sed in aquâ et sanguine; et spiritus testimonium dat, quoniam spiritus est veritas. Quia Tres sunt testes, spiritus, aqua, et sanguis; et hi Tres Unum sunt in Christo Jesu*[1]." The like reading of Facundus, Eucherius, and St. Austin, you have in the places cited above. These are Latins as late, or later, than Jerome ; for Jerome did not prevail with the churches of his own time to receive the testimony of "the Three in Heaven." And for them to know his version, and not receive his testimony, was in effect to condemn it.

[1] See also Ambrose in Luc. xxii. 10, and in his book, De iis qui mysteriis initiantur, cap. 4.

XV. And as for the Greeks, Cyril of Alexandria reads the text without this testimony in the xivth book of his Thesaurus, cap. 5 ; and again in his first book *De Fide ad Reginas*, a little after the middle ; and so does Oecumenius, a later Greek, in his commentary on this place of St. John's epistle. Also, Didymus Alexandrinus, in his commentary on the same passage, reads, " the Spirit, Water, and Blood," without mentioning " the Three in Heaven:" and so he doth in his book of the Holy Ghost, where he seems to omit nothing that he could find for his purpose : and so doth Gregory Nazianzen in his xxxviith oration concerning the Holy Ghost ; and also Nicetas in his commentary on Gregory Nazianzen's xlivth oration : And here it is further observable, that, as the Eusebians had contended, that " the Father, Son, and Holy Ghost" were not to be connumerated, because they were things of a different kind ; Nazianzen and Nicetas answer, that they might be connumerated, because St. John connumerates three things not substantial, namely, " the Spirit, the Water, and the Blood." By the objection of the Eusebians, it then appears that the testimony of " the Three in Heaven" was not in their books ; and by the answer of the Catholics it is as evident, that it was not in theirs ; for while they answer by instancing " the Spirit, Water, and Blood," they could not have missed of " the Father, the Word, and the Holy Ghost," had they been connumerated, and called one in the words immediately before; and to answer by instancing in these, would have been far more to their purpose, because it was the very thing in question. In like manner the Eunomians, in disputing against the Catholics, had objected, that the Holy Ghost is nowhere in Scripture conjoined with the Father and the Son, except in the form of baptism; which is as much as to say, that the testimony of " the Three in Heaven" was not in their books: and yet St. Basil[1], whilst he is very diligent in returning an answer to them, and perplexes himself in citing places, which are nothing to the purpose, does not produce this text of " the Three in Heaven," though it be the most obvious, and the only proper passage, had it been then in the Scriptures; and therefore he knew nothing of it. The objection of the Eunomians, and the answer of the Catholics, sufficiently show that it was in the books of neither party. Besides all this, the tenth epistle of Pope Leo, mentioned above, was that very famous epistle to Flavian, patriarch of Constantinople, against Eutyches which went about through all the churches, both Eastern and Western, being translated into Greek, and sent about in the East by Flavian. It was generally applauded in the West, and read in the council of Chalcedon, and there solemnly approved and subscribed by all the bishops; and in this epistle the text was thus cited: " *Et spiritus est qui*

[1] Lib. 5, adversus Eunomium sub finem.

testificatur, quoniam Christus est veritas; quia Tres sunt, qui testimonium dant, spiritus, aqua, et sanguis; et hi Tres Unum sunt." And by putting πνευμα (according to the Greek reading) for *Christus,* which is still the vulgar Latin, it was thus translated by the Greeks : "και το πνευμα εστιν το μαρτυρουν· επειδη το πνευμα εστιν ἡ αληθεια· τρεις γαρ εισιν οἱ μαρτυρουντες, το πνευμα, και το ὑδωρ, και το αἱμα, και οἱ τρεις το ἑν εισι." So then we have the reading, quoted by the Pope, owned in the West, and solemnly subscribed in the East by the fourth general council, and therefore it continued the public received reading in both the East and West, till after the age of that council.

XVI. So then the testimony of " the Three in Heaven," which, in the times of these controversies, would have been in everybody's mouth, had it been in their books, was wholly unknown to the churches of those ages. All that they could find in their books was the testimony of " the Water, the Spirit, and the Blood." Will you now say, that the testimony of " the Three in Heaven" was razed out of their books by the prevailing Arians? Yes, truly, those Arians were crafty knaves, that could conspire so cunningly and slily all the world over at once (as at the word of a Mithridates) in the latter end of the reign of the emperor Constantius, to get all men's books in their hands, and correct them without being perceived : ay, and conjurors too, to do it without leaving any blot or chasm in their books, whereby the knavery might be suspected and discovered ; and to wipe away the memory of it out of all men's brains, so that neither Athanasius, or anybody else, could afterwards remember that they had ever seen it in their books before ; and out of their own books too ; so that when they turned to the consubstantial faith, as they generally did in the West, soon after the death of Constantius, they could then remember no more of it than anybody else. Well, then, it was out of their books in Jerome's age, when he pretended it was in ; which is the point we are to prove ; and when anybody can show, that it was in their books before, it may be pertinent to consider that point also ; but till then we are only to inquire how, since it was out, it came into the copies that are now extant. For they that, without proof, accuse the heretics of corrupting books, and upon that pretence correct them at their pleasure without the authority of ancient manuscripts, as some learned men of the fourth and fifth centuries used to do, are falsaries by their own confession, and certainly need no other confutation. And therefore if this reading was once out, we are bound in justice to believe, that it was out from the beginning ; unless the razing of it out can be proved by some better argument than that of pretence and clamour.

XVII. Will you now say, that Jerome followed some copy different from any which the Greeks were acquainted with? This is to overthrow the authority of his version by making him depart from the received Greeks; and besides, it is contrary to what he himself seems to represent; for in his blaming not the vulgar Greek copies, but the Latin interpreters only, which were before his time, as if they had varied from the received Greek, he represents that he himself followed it. He does not excuse and justify himself for reading differently from the received Greek, to follow a private copy, but accuses former interpreters, as if, in leaving out the testimony of " the Three in Heaven," they had not followed the received Greek, as he did. And, therefore, since the Greeks knew nothing of this testimony, the authority of his version sinks; and that the rather, because he was then accused of corrupting the text, and could not persuade either the Greeks or the Latins of those times to receive his reading; for the Latins received it not till many years after his death; and the Greeks not till this present age, when the Venetians sent it amongst them in printed books; and their not receiving it was plainly to approve the accusation.

XVIII. The authority of this version being thus far discussed, it remains, that we consider the authority of the manuscripts wherein we now read the testimony of " the Three in Heaven." And by the best inquiry that I have been able to make, it is wanting in the manuscripts of all languages but the Latin. For, as we have shown, that the Æthiopic, Syriac, Arabic, Armenian, and Sclavonian versions, still in use in the several Eastern nations, Ethiopia, Egypt, Syria, Mesopotamia, Armenia, Muscovy, and some others, are strangers to this reading, and that it was anciently wanting also in the French; so I am told by those who have been in Turkey, that it is wanting to this day in the Greek manuscripts, which have been brought from those parts into the West; and that the Greeks, now that they have got it in print from the Venetians, when their manuscripts are objected against it, pretend that the Arians razed it out. A reading to be found in no manuscripts but the Latin, and not in the Latin before Jerome's age, as Jerome himself confesses, can be but of little authority : and this authority sinks, because we have already proved the reading spurious, by showing that it was heretofore unknown, both to the Western and the Eastern churches, in the times of the great controversy about the Trinity. But, however, for further satisfaction, we shall now give you an account of the Latin and Greek manuscripts; and show, first, how, in the dark ages, it crept into the Latin manuscripts out of Jerome's version ; and then how it lately crept out of the Latin into the printed Greek without the authority of manuscripts; those who first published it in Greek having never yet so much as seen it in any Greek manuscript.

XIX. That the vulgar Latin, now in use, is a

mixture of the old vulgar Latin, and of Jerome's version together, is the received opinion. Few of these manuscripts are above four or five hundred years old. The latest generally have the testimony of "the Three in Heaven:" the oldest of all usually want it, which shows that it has crept in by degrees. Erasmus notes it to be wanting in three very ancient ones, one of which was in the Pope's library at Rome, the other two were at Bruges; and he adds, that in another manuscript belonging to the library of the Minorites in Antwerp, the testimony of "the Three in Heaven" was noted in the margin in a newer hand. Peter Cholinus notes in the margin of his Latin edition of the Scriptures, printed anno Christi 1543 and 1544, that it was wanting in the most ancient manuscript of the Tugurine library. Dr. Gilbert Burnet has lately, in the first letter of his travels, noted it wanting in five other ones kept at Strasburg, Zurich, and Basil; one of which manuscripts he reckons about 1000 years old, and the other four about 800. F. Simon has noted it wanting in five others in the libraries of the king of France, Mons. Colbert, and the Benedictines of the Abbey of St. Germain's. An ancient and diligent collator of manuscripts, cited by Lucas Brugensis by the name of Epanorthotes, notes in general, that it was wanting in the ancient Latin manuscripts. Lucas himself, collating many Latin ones, notes it to be wanting in only *five*, that is, in the few old ones he had, his manuscripts being almost all of them new ones. For he praises[1] the Codex Lobiensis written anno Christi 1084, and the Codex Tornacensis written anno Christi 1105, as most ancient and venerable for their antiquity; and used others much more new, of which a great number was easily had; such as was the Codex Buslidianus, written anno Christi 1432, that is, but eight years before the invention of printing. The Lateran council, collected under Innocent the Third, anno Christi 1215, canon 2, mentions Joachim, the abbot, quoting the text in these words : " *Quoniam in canonicâ Johannis epistolâ [legitur,] Quia Tres sunt qui testimonium dant in cœlo, Pater, et Verbum, et Spiritus; et hi Tres Unum sunt: statimque subjungitur: Et Tres sunt qui testimonium dant in terrâ, Spiritus, Aqua, et Sanguis, et Tres Unum sunt: sicut in codicibus quibusdam invenitur.*" This was written by Joachim[2] in the papacy of Alexander the Third, that is, in or before the year 1180, and therefore this reading was then got but into some books ; for the words " *sicut in codicibus quibusdam invenitur*" refer as well to the first words of Joachim, " *quoniam in canonicâ Johannis epistolâ legitur,*" as to the text [*next*], "*statimque subjungitur;*" and more to the first than the text [*next*], because the first part of the citation was then but in some books, as appears by ancient manuscripts ; but the second part was in almost

---

[1] Lucas Brug. in calce annot.
[2] Vide Math. Paris Histor. Angl. A.D. 1179.

all: the words "*Tres Unum sunt*" being in all the books which wanted the testimony of "the Three in Heaven," and in most of those which had it; though afterwards left out in many, when branded by the schoolmen for Arian.

XX. But to go to the original of the corruption. Gregory the great [1] writes, that Jerome's version was in use in his time, and therefore no wonder if the testimony of "the Three in Heaven" began to be cited out of it before. Eugenius bishop of Carthage, in the seventh year of Hunneric king of the Vandals, anno Christi 484, in the summary of his faith exhibited to the king, cited it the first of any man, so far as I can find. A while after, Fulgentius, another African bishop, disputing against the same Vandals, cited it again, and backed it with the forementioned place of Cyprian, applied to the testimony of "the Three in Heaven." And so it is probable, that by that abused authority of Cyprian it began first in Afric, in the disputes with the ignorant Vandals, to get some credit; and thence at length crept into use. It occurs also frequently in Vigilius Tapsensis, another African bishop, contemporary to Fulgentius. In its defence, some allege earlier writers; namely, the first epistle of Pope Hyginus, the first epistle of Pope John II. the book of Idacius Clarus against Varimadus; and the book, *De unitâ Deitate Trinitatis*, ascribed to Athanasius. But Chiffletius, who published the works of

[1] Vide Walton's Prolegomena, x. 5.

Victor Vitensis and Vigilius Tapsensis, sufficiently proves the book against Varimadus to be
this Vigilius's, and erroneously ascribed to Idacius.   To the same Vigilius he asserts also the
book *De unitâ Deitate Trinitatis*.   Certainly
Athanasius was not its author.   All the epistles of
Hyginus, except the beginning and the end, and
the first part of the epistle of Pope John, wherein
the testimony of " the Three in Heaven " is cited,
are nothing else than fragments of the book
against Varimadus, described word by word by
some forger of decretal epistles, as may appear
by comparing them.   So then Eugenius is the
first upon record that quotes it.

XXI.   But though he set it on foot among the
Africans, yet I cannot find that it became of authority in Europe before the revival of learning
in the twelfth and thirteenth centuries.   In those
ages St. Barnard, the Schoolmen, Joachim, and
the Lateran council, spread it abroad, and scribes
began generally to insert it into the text; but in
such in Latin manuscripts and European writers,
as are ancienter than those times, it is scarce to
be met with.

XXII.   Now that it was inserted into the vulgar Latin out of Jerome's version, is manifest by
the manner how the vulgar Latin and that version
came to be mixed.   For it is agreed that the
Latines, after Jerome's version began to be of use,
noted out of it his corrections of the vulgar Latin in the margin of their books; and these the

transcribers afterwards inserted into the text. By this means, the old Latin has been so generally corrected, that it is nowhere to be found sincere. It is Jerome that we now read, and not the old vulgar Latin; and what wonder, if in Jerome we read the testimony of "the Three in Heaven?" For who that inserted the rest of Jerome into the text, would leave out such a passage for the Trinity, as this hath been taken to be?

XXIII. But to put the question out of dispute, there are footsteps of the insertion still remaining. For in some old manuscripts it has been found noted in the margin; in others, the various readings are such as ought to arise, by transcribing it out of the margin into the text. I shall only mention the three following varieties. Of the manuscripts which have not the testimony of "the Three in Heaven," some have the words *in terrâ*, in the eighth verse, but the most want it; which seems to proceed from hence, that some, before they allowed so great an addition to the text, as the testimony of "the Three in Heaven," noted only *in terrâ* in the margin of their books, to be inserted into the testimony of the Spirit, Water, and Blood. Of the manuscripts which have the testimony of "the Three in Heaven," some in the eighth verse have "*Hi Tres Unum sunt;*" others not. The reason of this seems to be, that of those who noted this testimony in the margin, some blotted out "*Et hi Tres Unum sunt*" in the eighth verse according to Jerome; and others did not. And, lastly, the testimony of "the Three in Heaven" is in most books set before the testimony of "the Three in earth;" in some, it is set after; so Erasmus notes two old books, in which it is set after; Lucas Brugensis a third; and Hesselius (if I misremember not) a fourth; and so Vigilius Tapsensis[1] sets it after; which seems to proceed from hence, that it was sometimes so noted in the margin, that the reader or transcriber knew not whether it were to come before or after. Now these discords in the Latin manuscripts, as they detract from the authority of the manuscripts, so they confirm to us, that the old vulgar Latin has in these things been tampered with, and corrected by Jerome's version.

XXIV. In the next place, I am to show how, and when, the testimony of "the Three in Heaven" crept out of the Latin into the Greek. Those who first printed the Greek Testament, did generally, in following their manuscripts, omit the testimony of "the Three in Heaven," except in Spain; for it was omitted in the first and second edition of Erasmus, anno Christi 1516 and 1519; in the edition of Francis Asulan, printed at Venice by Aldus, anno Christi 1518; in that of Nicholas Gerbelius, printed at Haganau, anno Christi 1521; and a little after, in that of Wolfius Cephalius, printed at Strasburg, anno Christi 1524; and again in 1526, in the Badian edition,

[1] Vigilius, libr. advers. Varimadum, cap. 5.

as Erasmus notes; and in that of Simon Colinæus at Paris, anno Christi 1534[1]. At the same time it was omitted in some editions of other Western languages, as in the Saxon and German editions of Luther; and in the Latin Tugurine editions of Peter Cholinus, anno Christi 1543 and 1544. The first edition in Greek, which has the testimony of "the Three in Heaven," was that of Cardinal Ximenes, printed at Complutum in Spain, in 1515; but not published before the year 1521. The Cardinal, in his edition, used the assistance of several divines, which he called together to Complutum, there founding an university, anno Christi 1517, or a little before. Two of those divines were Antonius Nebrissensis and Stunica. For Stunica then resided at Complutum, and in the preface[2] to a treatise he wrote against Erasmus, gives this testimony of himself:

[1] " In editis exemplaribus nonnullis non legi; ut in Aldinâ et Badianâ editione. Addo, nec in Græco Testamento Gerbelii Haganoæ, 1521; nec in Colinæi Parisiis edito."—*Gomarus in h. l.*

[2] " Cum præsertim, si quisquam alius, et nos quoque his de rebus, nostro quodam jure, judicium ferre possumus. [Quippe] qui non paucos annos in sanctis scripturis Veteris et Novi Testamenti, Hebraicè, Græcè, et Latinè perlegendis consumpserimus; ac Hebraica, Græcaque ipsa divinarum literarum exemplaria cum Latinis codicibus diligentissimè contulerimus. Longâ igitur lectione ac experientiâ jampridem edocti, quantum tralationi huic ecclesiasticæ Novi Testamenti deferendum sit, ni fallor, optimè novi."—*Hæc Stunica in proem. libri sui.*

"That he had spent some years in reading the holy Scriptures in Hebrew, Greek, and Latin; and had diligently collated the Hebrew and Greek exemplars with the Latin copies." This book, displeasing the cardinal, was not printed till after his death; and then it came forth at Complutum, anno Christi 1520. The year before, one Lee, an Englishman, writ also against Erasmus; and both Stunica and Lee, amongst other things, reprehended him for omitting the testimony of "the Three in Heaven." Afterwards Erasmus, finding the Spaniards, and some others of the Roman church, in a heat against him, printed this testimony in his third edition, anno Christi 1522, representing, "That in his former editions he had printed the text as he found it in his manuscripts; but now there being found in England one manuscript which had the testimony of 'the Three in Heaven,' he had inserted it, according to that manuscript; for avoiding the calumnies raised against him." And so it continued in his two following editions. And at length Robert Stephens, anno Christi 1550, reprinted Erasmus's edition, with some few alterations and various lections, taken out of the Complutensian edition, and fifteen Greek manuscripts, which he named after the numeral letters a, β, γ, δ, ϵ, &c., putting a for the Complutensian edition, and β, γ, δ, ϵ, &c. for the manuscripts in order; and noting in the margin, that the testimony of "the Three in Heaven" was wanting in the seven manuscripts, δ, ε, ζ, θ, ι, ια, ιγ.   Whence Beza[1] tells us, that he had read it in the rest.   His words are, " *Legit Hieronymus, legit Erasmus in Britannico codice, et in Complutensi editione. Legimus et nos in nonnullis Roberti nostri veteribus libris.*" And this is the original and authority of the printed editions.   For these are the editions ever since followed by all the West; and of late years propagated by the Venetian presses into Greece; and nothing further, that I know of, has been discovered in any manuscripts in favour of these editions.

XXV. Now to pull off the vizard, I cannot but, in the first place, extremely complain of Beza's want of modesty and caution in expressing himself[2].   In the preface to his annotations, describing what helps he had in composing his first edition, he tells us, "That he had the annotations of Valla, Stapulensis, and Erasmus, and the writings of the ancients and moderns collated by himself; and out of Stephens's library, the exemplar which Stephens had collated with about twenty-five manuscripts, almost all of which were printed."   He should have said seventeen; for that number he puts in other places, and in his

[1] Beza in hunc locum.

[2] "Non desunt, qui Bezam nimis audacem fuisse judicant, dum à receptâ lectione sæpiùs sine necessitate recedit; et unius, interdum nullius, codicis authoritate fretus, prætoriam exercet potestatem, ex conjecturis mutando et interpolando textum sacrum pro libitu."—*Walton. Prolegom.* iv. *sect.* 15, *in Bibl. Polyglot.*

annotations cites no more. So then he had the collations of two more manuscripts than Stephens has given us in print. And this was all his furniture. The original manuscripts he does not here pretend to have; nor could he have them; for they were not Stephens's manuscripts, but belonged to several libraries in France and Italy. The manuscript β Stephens himself never saw; but had only various lections collected out of it by his friends in Italy. The manuscripts γ, δ, ε, ϛ, ζ, η, ι, ιε, were not Stephens's, but belonged to the library of the king of France, to whom Stephens was printer. The other six books, θ, ια, ιβ, ιγ, ιδ, ιϛ, Stephens had not out of his own library, but borrowed them for a time from several places to collate, his friends studying to promote the design of his edition. And yet Beza in his annotations, when he would favour any text, cites the collations of Stephens in such a manner, as if he had the very original manuscripts at Geneva before his eyes. And where Stephens does not cite various lections, there he reckons, that in the text of Stephens's collated books he read all the manuscripts. So in Mark vi. 11, where Stephens notes a certain period to be wanting in the manuscript copies β and η, Beza saith, " *Hæc periodus in omnibus exemplaribus Græcis legitur, exceptis secundo et octavo.*" In the Acts xiii. 33, because Stephens had noted no various lections, Beza affirms of the Greek text, " *Ita scriptum invenimus in omnibus vetustis codicibus.*" In 1 John iv. 3, where

Stephens is silent, Beza speaks; " *Sic legitur in omnibus Græcis exemplaribus, quæ quidem mihi inspicere licuit.*" In James i. 22, where Stephens is again silent, Beza tells us of the word μονον, " *Ego in omnibus nostris vetustis libris inveni.*" And so, where Stephens in the margin had noted the testimony of " the Three in Heaven " to be wanting in seven manuscripts, he thinks that, in reading the text of Stephens's collated book, he reads it in the rest; and so tells us, " *Legimus et nos in nonnullis Roberti Stephani codicibus.*" This he did in the first edition of his annotations. Afterwards, when he had got two real manuscripts, the Claromontan, and that which at length he presented to the University of Cambridge (in both which the canonical epistles are wanting); in the epistle to his fourth edition, in reckoning up the books he then used, he puts only these two, and the seventeen of Stephens; and in his fifth edition he writes summarily, that he used nineteen manuscripts, joining with those two real ones the collations of Stephens, as if in those he had seventeen others; which sufficiently explains his way of speaking in his annotations. But whilst he had not the manuscripts themselves to read with his own eyes, it was too hard and unwarrantable a way of speaking to tell us, " *Legimus et nos in nonnullis Roberti Stephani codicibus;*" and therefore, in his later editions, he corrects himself, and tells us, only, that the reading doth " *extare in nonnullis Stephani veteribus libris.*" Thus Beza

argues from Stephens's book of collations; and
the same inference has been made by Lucas Brugensis and others, ever since, from Stephens's
fore-mentioned edition of that book. "For," say
they, "Stephens had fifteen manuscripts in all,
and found the testimony of 'the Three in Heaven'
wanting but in seven; and therefore it was in the
other eight; and so being found in the greater
part of his manuscripts, has the authority and
manuscripts on its side." Thus they argue; and
this is the great argument by which the printed
Greek has hitherto been justified.

XXVI. But if they please to consider the business a little better, they will find themselves
very much mistaken. For though Stephens had
fifteen manuscripts in all, yet all of them did not
contain all the Greek Testament. Four of them,
noted γ, ς, $\iota\beta$, $\iota\delta$, had each of them the four
Gospels only. Two, noted β, η, contained only
the Gospels and the Acts of the Apostles. One,
noted $\iota\varsigma$, contained the Apocalypse only. One,
noted $\iota\epsilon$, had only the Apocalypse, with St Paul's
Epistles to the Corinthians, Galatians, Ephesians,
Philippians, and Colossians. The other seven,
noted δ, ϵ, ζ, θ, ι, ιa, $\iota\gamma$, contained both St. Paul's
Epistles and the canonical ones, besides some
other books; namely, the manuscript ζ contained
the Epistles and Gospels; the manuscripts ι, ιa,
$\iota\gamma$, the Epistles and Acts of the Apostles; and
the manuscripts δ, ϵ, θ, the Epistles, Gospels,
and Acts. And this any one may gather, by

noting what manuscripts the various lections are
cited out of, in every book of the New Testament.
For in the various lections of the canonical epistles, and those to the Thessalonians, Timothy,
Titus, and the Hebrews, are found these seven
manuscripts, δ, ϵ, ζ, θ, ι, ιa, $\iota \gamma$, everywhere
cited, and no more than these.   The same also,
and no more, are cited in the epistles to the
Thessalonians, Timothy, Titus, and the Hebrews;
one numeral error (whether of the scribe or typo-
grapher) excepted.   Stephens therefore did collect various lections of the Epistles out of only
these seven manuscripts, δ, ϵ, ζ, θ, ι, ιa, $\iota \gamma$; and
in all these seven he found the testimony of " the
Three in Heaven" to be wanting; as you may
see noted in the margin of his edition.

XXVII. And that this testimony was wanting
in all Stephens's manuscripts, is apparent also
by its being generally wanting in the manuscripts
which are now extant in France.   For Father
Simon [1] tells us, " That after a diligent search in
the library of the king of France, and in that also
of Monsieur Colbert, he could not find it in any
one manuscript; though he consulted seven manuscripts in the king's library, and one in Colbert's."   And because Stephens had some of his
various lections from Italy, I will add, that a
gentleman, who, in his travels, had consulted
twelve manuscripts in several libraries in Italy,
assured me that he found it wanting in them all.

[1] Simon's Critical History of the New Test. chap. xviii.

One of the twelve was that most ancient and most famous manuscript in the Pope's library, written in capital letters.

XXVIII. So then the authority of the printed books rests only upon the authority of the editions of Erasmus and Cardinal Ximenes. But seeing that Erasmus omitted it in his two first editions, and inserted it unwillingly, against the authority of his manuscripts, in his three last; the authority of these three can be none at all. When Lee, upon Erasmus's putting forth his second edition, fell foul upon him for leaving out the testimony of " the Three in Heaven," Erasmus[1] answered, "That he had consulted more than seven Greek manuscripts, and found it wanting in them all; and that if he could have found it in any one manuscript, he would have followed that in favour of the Latin." Hence notice was sent to Erasmus out of England, that it was in a manuscript there; and thereupon to avoid[2] their calumnies (as he saith) he printed it in his following editions; notwithstanding that he suspected that manuscript

---

[1] " Dicam mihi diversis temporibus plura fuisse exemplaria quàm septem [scilicet Græca] ; nec in ullo horum repertum, quod in nostris [scilicet Latinis] legitur. Quod si contigisset unum exemplar, in quo fuisset, quod nos legimus, nimirum illinc adjecissem, quod in cæteris aberat. Id quia non contigit, quod solum licuit, feci ; indicavi quid in Græcis codicibus minus esset."—*Hæc Erasmus contra Leum, in hunc locum.*

[2] " Ex hoc igitur codice Britannico reposuimus, quod in nostris dicebatur deesse ; ne cui sit ansa calumniandi. Quan-

to be a new one, corrected by the Latin.   But since, upon inquiry, I cannot learn that they in England ever heard of any such manuscript, but from Erasmus; and since he was only told of such a manuscript, in the time of the controversy between him and Lee, and never saw it himself, I cannot forbear to suspect, that it was nothing but a trick put upon him by some of the Popish clergy, to try if he would make good what he had offered, the printing of the testimony of " the Three in Heaven" by the authority of one Greek copy, and thereby to get it into his edition[1]. Greek manuscripts of the Scripture are things of value, and do not use to be thrown away ; and such a manuscript, for the testimony of "the Three in Heaven," would have made a greater noise than the rest have done against it.   Let those who have such a manuscript, at length tell us where it is.

XXIX. So also let them, who insist upon the edition of cardinal Ximenes, tell us by what manuscript he printed this testimony ; or, at least, where any such manuscript of good note is to be seen ; for till then I must take the liberty

quam et hunc suspicor, et Latinorum codices, fuisse castiga-tum.   Posteaquam enim concordiam inierunt cum ecclesiâ Romanâ, studuerunt et hac in parte cum Romanis consentire."
—*Erasmi Annotation. in hunc locum ; editio tertia, et sequen.*

[1] "Versiculus 1 Joan. v. 7, in Syriacâ, ut et vetustissimis Græcis exemplaribus, nostro Alexandrino, aliis manuscriptis Græcis, quos contulimus, non reperitur."—*Walton. Prole-gomena,* xiv. 23, *in Bibl. Polyglot.*

to believe, that he printed nothing else than a translation out of the Latin, and that for these reasons.

First : Because in the preface to his edition
of the New Testament we are told, that this Testament was printed after the manuscripts taken
out of the Pope's library ; and these the cardinal
only borrowed[1] thence, and therefore returned
them back so soon as his edition was finished.
And Caryophilus some time after, by the Pope's
command, collating the Vatican manuscripts,
found the testimony of "the Three in Heaven"
wanting in them all. I do not say but that the
cardinal had other manuscripts ; but these were
the chief, and the only ones he thought worth
while to tell his reader of.

Secondly : I startle at the marginal note in this
place of the cardinal's edition. For it is beside
the use of this edition, to put notes in the margin
of the Greek text. I have not found it done above
thrice in all this edition of the New Testament ;
and therefore there must be something extraordinary ; and that, in respect of the Greek, because
it is in the margin of this text. In 1 Corinth. xv.
there is noted in this margin a notable variation
in the Greek reading. In Matthew vi. 13, where
they, in their edition, recede from the Greek copies, and correct it by the Latin, they make a

[1] "Accivit è Vaticanâ Romæ Bibliothecâ, bonâ cum Leo-
nis X. pontificis maximi veniâ ;"—as Gasper Bellerus, in his
epistle prefixed to the Quinquagena of Antonius Nabrissen-
sis, expresses it,

marginal note to justify their doing so; and so here, where the testimony of "the Three in Heaven" is generally wanting in the Greek copies, they make a third marginal note, to secure themselves from being blamed for printing it. Now in such a case as this, there is no question but they would make the best defence they could ; and yet they do not tell of any various lections in the Greek manuscripts, nor produce any one Greek manuscript on their side, but run to the authority of Thomas Aquinas[1]. The Greek manuscripts have the text thus : " For there are Three that bear record, the Spirit, the Water, and the Blood; and these Three are One." In many of the Latin manuscripts, the words "these Three are One" are here omitted, and put only at the end of the

---

[1] The marginal note is this : " Sanctus Thomas, in expositione secundæ decretalis de summâ Trinitate et Fide Catholicâ, tractans istum passum contra Abbatem Joachim, viz. 'Tres sunt, qui testimonium dant in cœlo, Pater, Verbum, et Spiritus Sanctus,' dicit ad literam verba sequentia :—' Et ad insinuendam unitatem trium personarum subditur, et Hi Tres Unum sunt ;' quandoquidem dicitur propter essentiæ unitatem. Sed hoc Joachim perversè trahere volens ad unitatem charitatis et consensûs, inducebat consequentem auctoritatem. Nam subditur ibidem, 'Et Tres sunt, qui testimonium dant in terrâ, Spiritus Sanctus, Aqua, et Sanguis :' et in quibusdam libris additur, 'et hi Tres Unum sunt.' Sed hoc in veris exemplaribus non habetur ; sed dicitur esse appositum ab Hæreticis Arianis ad pervertendum intellectum sanum auctoritatis præmissæ de unitate essentiæ Trium Personarum." Hæc Beatus Thomas, ubi supra.

testimony of "the Three in Heaven," before that of "the Spirit, Water, and Blood:" in others they are put after both testimonies. In the Complutensian edition they follow the former copies, and justify their doing so, by the authority of Thomas Aquinas. "Thomas," say they, "in treating of the Three which bear witness in Heaven, teaches, that the words 'these Three are One' are subjoined for insinuating the unity of the essence of the Three persons. And whereas one Joachim interpreted this unity to be only in *love* and *consent*, it being thus said of the Spirit, Water, and Blood, in some copies, 'these Three are One';" Thomas replied, "That this last clause is not extant in the true copies; but was added by the Arians for perverting the sense." Thus far this annotation. Now this plainly respects the Latin copies (for Thomas understood not Greek), and therefore part of the design of this annotation is to set right the Latin reading. But this is not the main design. For so the annotation should have been set in the margin of the Latin version. Its being set in the margin of the Greek text, shows that its main design is to justify the Greek by the Latin thus rectified and confirmed. Now to make Thomas thus, in a few words, do all the work, was very artificial; and in Spain, where Thomas is of apostolic authority, might pass for a very judicious and substantial defence of the printed Greek. But to us Thomas Aquinas is no Apostle. We are seeking for the authority of Greek manuscripts.

A third reason why I conceive the Complutensian Greek to have been in this place a translation from the Latin, is, because Stunica (who as
I told you, was one of the divines employed by
the Cardinal in this edition, and at that very time
wrote against Erasmus) when, in his objections,
he comes to this text of the testimony of "the
Three in Heaven," he cites not one Greek manuscript for it against Erasmus; but argues wholly
from the authority of the Latin. On the contrary,
he sets down, by way of concession, the common
reading of the Greek mannscripts (as well as his
own, and that of others) in these words, "ὅτι
τρεις εισιν οἱ μαρτυρουντες· το πνευμα, και το
ὑδωρ, και το αἱμα· και οἱ τρεις εις το ἑν εισι:"
and then condemns them altogether without ex-
ception; and justifies the Latin against them by
the authority of Jerome. "Know," saith he,
"that in this place the Greek manuscripts are
most evidently corrupted; but ours (that is, the
Latin ones) contain the truth itself, as they are
translated from the first original: which is manifest by the prologue of St. Jerome upon the
Epistles, &c."[1]. And this prologue (which he
goes on to cite at length, and of which we gave

[1] "Sciendum est, hoc loco codices apertissimè esse cor-
ruptos; nostros verò veritatem ipsam, ut à primâ origine
traducti sunt, continere; quod ex prologo B. Hieronymi super
Epistolas manifestè apparet. Ait enim, ' Quæ si sicut ab eis
digestæ sunt; ita quoque ab interpretibus fideliter in Latinum
verterentur eloquium,' " &c.—*Hæc Stunica in hunc locum.
Ejus Liber exstat in Criticor. vol.* ix.

you an account above) is all he argues in favour
of the testimony of "the Three in Heaven." In
other places of Scripture, where he had Greek
manuscripts on his side, he produces them readily.
So 1 Thessalonians ii. 7, " *Ita quidem legitur,*"
says he, "*in Græcis codicibus quos ego viderim.*"

In James i. 11, he saith, " *Sciendum in omni-*
bus Græcis codicibus πορειαιϲ *hîc legi per* ει *di-*
phthongum." In 1 Thessalonians v. 23, he saith,
"*Cum in Græcis exemplaribus quotquot sunt,* ὁλο-
κληρον, *et in Latinis* integer *hîc legatur, perne-*
mine discrepante, nescio cur Erasmus dixerit," &c.
In Philipp. iv. 9, "*Si quidem in omnibus,*" saith he,
"*Græcis codicibus,* ταυτα λογιζεσθε *hîc legitur; ne-*
que Græci sunt libri, qui πρασσετε *hoc loco, neque*
Latini, qui agite ; *nisi mendosos utriusque, linguæ*
codices, cum hæc commentaretur Erasmus, perlegit."
After this manner does Stunica produce the manuscripts used in the Complutensian edition, when
they make for him; and here he produces them too,
but it is for Erasmus against himself. " Know,"
saith he, "that in this place the Greek manuscripts are most evidently corrupted." In other
places, if he hath but one manuscript on his side,
he produces it magnificently enough; as the Codex
Rhodiensis in his discourses upon 2 Corinthians
ii. 3, James i. 22, 2 Peter ii. 2, and other texts.
Here he produces all the manuscripts against himself, without excepting so much as one. And
hence Erasmus, in his answer to Stunica, gloried
in the consent of the Spanish manuscripts with

his own; and Sanctius Caranza, another of the Complutensian divines, in his defence of Stunica, written presently after, had nothing to reply in this point. Neither could Sepulveda, or the Spanish monks who next undertook the controversy, find one Greek manuscript, which here made against Erasmus. Neither had Marchio Valesius better success, though on that occasion he collated sixteen Greek manuscripts, eight whereof belonged to the king of Spain's library, and the other eight to other libraries of Spain: and he did it on purpose to collect out of them whatever he could meet with in favour of the present vulgar Latin. Neither did the reprinting of the Complutensian Bible by Arias Montanus produce the notice of any such manuscript; though, on that occasion, many manuscripts, as well Greek as Latin, fetched from Complutum and other places, were collated by Arias, Lucas Brugensis, Canter, and others.

XXX. So then, to sum up the argument, the Complutensian divines did sometimes correct the Greek by the Latin, without the authority of any Greek manuscript, as appears by their practice in Matthew vi. 13; and therefore their printing the testimony of "the Three in Heaven" is no evidence that they did it by a manuscript, but, on the contrary, for want of one, they contented themselves with the authority of Thomas Aquinas; and Stunica confessed that they had none. Nor has all the zeal for this text been able since to discover one either in Spain, or anywhere else.

XXXI. And now you may understand whence it is, that the Complutensian edition, and the reading of the pretended English manuscript, set down by Erasmus in his annotations, differ so much from one another; for the Complutensian edition has the text thus; "Ὅτι τρεις εισιν οἱ μαρτυρουντες εν τῳ ουρανῳ· ὁ πατηρ, ὁ λογος, και το ἁγιον πνευμα· και οἱ τρεις εις το ἑν εισι. και τρεις εισιν οἱ μαρτυρουντες επι της γης, το πνευμα, και το ὑδωρ, και το αἱμα." The pretended English manuscript thus; "Ὅτι τρεις εισιν οἱ μαρτυρουντες εν τῳ ουρανῳ, πατηρ, λογος, και πνευμα· και οὑτοι οἱ τρεις ἑν εισιν. και τρεις μαρτυρουντες εν τῃ γῃ, πνευμα, και ὑδωρ, και αἱμα." The differences are too great to spring from the bare errors of scribes, and arise rather from the various translations of the place, out of Latin into Greek, by two several persons.

XXXII. But whilst these two readings, by their discord, confute one another, the readings of the real Greek manuscripts by their agreement confirm one another as much. For Caryophilus, who by the command of Pope Urban the Eighth, collated the Vatican and other manuscripts, borrowed out of the principal libraries in Rome, found one common reading in them all, without the testimony of "the Three in Heaven;" as you may see in those his collations, printed in 1673 by Peter Possinus, in the end of his Catena of the Greek Fathers upon Mark. He met with eight manuscripts in all upon the epistles, and notes their reading thus: "1 Joan. v. 7, Manuscripti octo (omnes nempe) legunt, Ὁτι τρεις εισιν οἱ μαρτυρουντες, το πνευμα, και το ὑδωρ, και το αἱμα· και οἱ τρεις εις το ἑν εισι." "Porro totus septimus versus hujus capitis desideratur in octo manuscriptis codicibus Grӕcis," &c. Thus Caryophilus.

XXXIII. The very same reading Erasmus, in his annotations on this place, gives us of all his manuscripts, which were more than seven; and so doth Stephens of all his seven, without noting any various lections in them. Only the comma, which in Stephens's edition is, surely by mistake, set after ουρανψ, is to be put in its right place. The very same reading does Stunica also, in his book against Erasmus, note out of the manuscript he had seen in Spain, as was seen above. Nor does Valesius, in his collection of the sixteen Spanish manuscripts, note any various lections in this text. The same reading exactly have also the manuscripts in England; namely, that most ancient and famous one in the king's library, which was conveyed thither from Egypt through Greece, and published in Walton's Polyglott Bible; and the four at Oxford, viz. that in New College, and that in Magdalen College, both very old, and two in Lincoln College; and four or five other ancient ones lately collated at Oxford, in order to a new impression of the Greek Testament, as I am informed. The very same reading have also the three manuscripts of Monsieur Petavius Gachon, a senator of Paris, whose various lections, collected by his son John Gachon, were printed in the Oxford edition of the New Testament, anno Christi 1675. The same reading, without any variation, is published by Francis Asulan in his edition, printed anno Christi 1518, by Aldus at Venice, out of the manuscripts of those parts. The same reading Œcumenius, six hundred years ago, found in the manuscripts of Greece; as you may see in the text of his commentary on this epistle of St. John. The same reading also Cyril of Alexandria met with in the manuscripts of Egypt, above eleven hundred years ago; as you may see in his citations of the text; both in his Thesaurus, lib. xiv. cap. 5; and in his first book *De Fide ad Reginas*; excepting that in the latter of these two citations the paricle ειϲ is omitted; and μαρτυρουσι written for οἱ μαρτυρουντεϲ. And that the very same reading was also in the manuscripts of the first ages, may be gathered from the conformity of this reading to all the ancient versions.

XXXIV. It may seem by what has been hitherto said, that this testimony is not to be found in the Greek manuscripts. Epanorthotes[1], whom

---

[1] "Habuimus ab Hunnæo,—id quod maximi facimus, MS. Bibl. correctorium ab incerto auctore, quem Epanorthotem, aut correctorem fere vocamus, magnâ diligentiâ, ac fide contextum, secuto uti oportet antiquos nostræ editionis codices,

Lucas Brugensis describes to be an ancient, accurate, full, and industrious collator of manuscripts, found it wanting in all those he met with. " *Epanorthotes*," saith Lucas, " *deesse hæc eadem Græcis libris, et antiquis Latinis annotat.*" Nor have other collators made a further discovery to this day. Lee, Stunica, and the rest in England, Spain, Flanders, France, and Italy, who conspired against Erasmus, could find nothing in the manuscripts of those parts against him ; if that Phœnix be excepted, which once appeared to somebody somewhere in England, but could never since be seen. Hesselius[1], about the year 1565, pro-

eosque cum Hebræis, Græcis, et veterum patrum commentariis sedulo collatos ; qui liber ad Genesin viii. 7. latius à nobis descriptus est." Hæc Lucas ; qui ad Genesin viii. 7, dixit hunc librum multis annis scriptum, et pluribus fortè compositum. Dein, loco ex eo citato, pergit. Ad quæ dici quid possit ? An quod libro fidendum non sit ? Non hoc dicet, qui evolverit ; quæ namque à nostri seculi scriptoribus ex MSS. codicibus collectæ sunt variæ lectiones, omnes propemodum in eo comperimus ; et ad fontes fideliter examinatas deprehendimus. *Scripsit hæc Lucas,* anno 1579 ; "unde sequitur correctorium ante disputationes Erasmicas de testibus in cœlo elaboratum esse."

[1] Hesselius in hunc locum ait ; "Manuscripti Græci fere omnes sic se habent : ' Quoniam Tres sunt, qui testimonium dant in terrâ, Spiritus, Aqua, et Sanguis, et hi Tres Unum sunt;' nullâ factâ mentione triplicis testimonii de cœlo ' Patris, Verbi, et Spiritûs Sancti.' " Dein codices aliter legentes describendo sic pergit ; "Nostro tempore duo Græci codices manuscripti reperti sunt ; unus in Angliâ, et alter in Hispaniâ ; quorum uterque hoc loco testimonium habet ' Patris, Verbi, et Spiritûs Sancti.' "

fessor of divinity at Lovain, in his commentary on
this place, ingenuously confesses it wanting in
all the Greek manuscripts then known, except
two, the one in Spain, the other in England;
meaning those by which the Complutensian divines and Erasmus printed it. Which two we
have shown to be none at all; unless one Annius
dug up one in England. Since that time nothing
further has been produced, besides the imaginary
books of dreaming Beza. And yet I will not say,
but that it may hereafter be found in some Greek
copies. For in the times of the holy war, the
Latines had much to do in the East. They were
long united to the Greek church; they made Latin
patriarchs of Jerusalem and Antioch; they reigned
at Constantinople over the Greeks from the year
1204, for above fifty years together; and during
this their kingdom, in the year 1215, was assembled the Lateran council, consisting of four hundred and fifteen bishops, Greeks and Latins
together; and therein the testimony of "the Three
in Heaven" was quoted out of some of the Latin
manuscripts, as we told you above. All which
might occasion some Greeks, as well as Latins, to
note it in the margins of their books; and hence
insert it into the text in transcribing. For this is
most certain, that some Greek manuscripts have
been corrected by the Latin ones. Such a book
Erasmus[1] tells us, that he "once met with, and

[1] "Hic obiter illud incidit admonendum esse Græcorum
quosdam Novi Testamenti codices ad Latina exemplaria emen-

that there was such another in the Pope's library."
He suspected also that book in England, out of
which he printed the testimony of "the Three in
Heaven," to be of the same kind ; though I rather
think it was none at all ; unless some falsary of
that age were at the pains to transcribe one or
two of St. Paul's epistles. Such another book
was one of those, out of which Valesius collected
his various lections. Whence Mariana, into
whose hands the manuscript book of those lections fell, tells us, that for that reason, in his annotations on the New Testament, he used those
lections but sparingly and cautiously. And that
Valesius did meet with such a corrected manuscript, appears by the lections themselves. For
in the Apocalypse xviii. 17, where the Greek
reads επι τοπον ; and the Latin translates *in locum*,
and by the error of one letter *in lacum*, as the
books now have it ; some Grecian has here corrected this book by the Latin, and written επι
λιμνην ; as it is in the lections of Valesius, taken
out of this. Again, in the Apocalypse ix. 11,
where the Latin translation, in expounding the
names *Abaddon et Apollyon*, adds, *Et Latinè*

datos. Id factum est in fœdere Græcorum cum Romanâ ecclesiâ ; quod fœdus testatur Bulla, quæ dicitur Aurea ; visum
est enim et hoc ad firmandam concordiam pertinere. Et nos
olim in hujusmodi codicem incidimus ; et talis adhuc dicitur
adservari in Bibliothecâ Pontif. Verum ex his corrigere nostros est Lesbiam, ut aiunt, admovere regulam."—*Erasmus ad
Lectorem. Editio 5ta Novi Testamenti.*

habens nomen exterminans; Valesius notes the reading in his Greek copy to be ρωμαιϲι εχων ονο-μα εξτερμιναυϲ; which certainly is a translation of the Latin. Again, in the Apocalypse xxi. 12, where the Greek has αγγελουϲ, and some ancient Latin copies, *angelos,* but the far greater part of the Latin copies at present have *angulos;* Valesius, in his manuscript, reads γωνιαϲ. So in the Apocalypse xix. 6, where the Greek is οχλου πολλου, the Latin, *turbæ magnæ;* and in the later copies, *tubæ magnæ;* Valesius, in his manuscript, reads ϲαλπιγγοϲ μεγαληϲ. In Hebrews xiii. 2, for ελα-θον, *latuerunt;* and in later copies, *placuerunt,* Valesius reads ηρεσαν: and in 1 Peter iii. 8, for το δε τελοϲ, *in fine,* and by an error *in fide,* Valesius reads εν τη πιϲει δε. These, and such like instances, put the thing out of dispute. Now, though Valesius found not the testimony of " the Three in Heaven" in this manuscript; and Erasmus tells us, that he never saw it in any Greek manuscript; and, by consequence, not in that corrected one which fell into his hands; yet it may have crept out of the Latin into some other books, not yet taken notice of; and even in some manuscripts, which, in other places, have not been corrected by the Latin, it may possibly have been inserted by some of the Greek bishops of the Lateran council, where the testimony of " the Three in Heaven " was read. And therefore he that shall hereafter meet with it in any book, ought first, before he insist upon the authority of that book, to examine whether it has not been corrected by the Latin ; and whether it be ancienter than the Lateran council, and empire of the Latins in Greece ; for if it be liable to either of these two exceptions, it can signify nothing to produce it.

XXXV. Having given you the history of the controversy, I shall now confirm all that I have said from the sense of the text itself. For, without the testimony of " the Three in Heaven," the sense is good and easy, as you may see by the following paraphrase inserted in the text in a different character.

" WHO IS HE THAT OVERCOMETH THE WORLD, BUT HE THAT BELIEVETH THAT JESUS IS THE SON OF GOD ? that Son spoken of in the Psalms, where he saith, ' Thou art my Son ; this day have I begotten thee.' THIS IS HE THAT, after the Jews had long expected him, CAME, first in a mortal body BY baptism of WATER, AND then in an immortal one by shedding his BLOOD upon the cross, and rising again from the dead ; NOT BY WATER ONLY, BUT BY WATER AND BLOOD ; being the Son of God, as well by his resurrection from the dead (Acts xiii. 33.), as by his supernatural birth of the Virgin (Luke i. 35.). AND IT IS THE SPIRIT also, THAT, together with the water and blood, BEARETH WITNESS of the truth of his coming ; BECAUSE THE SPIRIT IS TRUTH ; and so a fit and unexceptionable witness. FOR THERE ARE THREE THAT BEAR RECORD of his coming ; THE SPIRIT, which he promised to send, and

which was since shed forth upon us in the form
of cloven tongues, and in various gifts; THE
baptism of WATER, wherein God testified, 'This
is my beloved Son;' AND THE shedding of his
BLOOD, accompanied with his resurrection, whereby he became the most faithful martyr or witness
of this truth. AND THESE THREE, the spirit, the
baptism, and passion of Christ, AGREE IN witnessing ONE and the same thing, namely, that
the Son of God is come; and, therefore, their
evidence is strong: for the law requires but two
consenting witnesses, and here we have three.
AND IF WE RECEIVE THE WITNESS OF MEN, THE
threefold WITNESS OF GOD, which he bare of his
Son, by declaring at his baptism, 'This is my
beloved Son;' by raising him from the dead, and
by pouring out his spirit on us, IS GREATER; and
therefore ought to be more readily received.''

XXXVI. Thus is the sense plain and natural,
and the argument full and strong; but if you insert the testimony of "the Three in Heaven," you
interrupt and spoil it. For the whole design of
the apostle being here to prove to men by witness the truth of Christ's coming, I would ask
how the testimony of "the Three in Heaven"
makes to this purpose. If their testimony be
not given to men, how does it prove to them the
truth of Christ's coming? If it be, how is the
testimony in heaven distinguished from that on
earth? It is the same spirit which witnesses in
heaven and in earth. If in both cases it witnesses

to us men, wherein lies the difference between
its witnessing in heaven, and its witnessing in
earth?   If, in the first case, it does not witness
to men, to whom does it witness?   And to what
purpose?   And how does its witnessing make to
the design of St. John's discourse?   Let them
make good sense of it who are able.   For my
part, I can make none. If it be said that we are
not to determine what is Scripture, and what not,
by our private judgements ; I confess it in places,
not controverted ; but in disputable places, I love
to take up with what I can best understand.   It
is the temper of the hot and superstitious part of
mankind, in matters of religion, ever to be fond
of mysteries ; and for that reason, to like best
what they understand least. Such men may use
the apostle John as they please ; but I have that
honour for him, as to believe that he wrote good
sense ; and therefore take that sense to be *his*,
which is the best ; especially since I am defended
in it by so great authority.   For I have on my
side the authority of the Fourth General Council,
and, so far as I know, of all the churches in all
ages, except the modern Latin, and such others
as have lately been influenced by them ; and that
also of all the old versions, and Greek manuscripts,
and ancient Latin ones ; and nothing against me,
but the authority of Jerome, and the credulity
and heat of his followers.

For to tell us of other manuscripts, without
ever letting us know in what libraries they were

to be seen; to pretend manuscripts, which, since
their first discovery, could never be heard of; nor
were then seen by persons whose names and
credit we know; is plainly to impose upon the
learned world, and ought not to pass any longer
for plain dealing. The Spaniards tell us plainly
that they followed the Latin, and by the authority
of Thomas left out the clause, " And these Three
are One," in the eighth verse, as inserted by the
Arians. And yet St. Ambrose, St. Austin, Eucherius, and other Latins, in the Arian age,
gathered the unity of the Deity from this clause ;
and the omission of it is now, by printing it, ac-
knowledged to be an erroneous correction. The
manuscript in England wanted the same clause,
and therefore, if there was any such manuscript,
it was a corrected one, like the Spanish edition,
and the manuscript of Valesius. Erasmus, who
printed the triple testimony in heaven by that
English manuscript, never saw it; tells us it was
a new one ; suspected its sincerity ; and accused
it publicly in his writings on several occasions,
for several years together ; and yet his adversaries
in England never answered his accusation ; never
endeavoured to satisfy him and the world about
it; did not so much as let us know where the
record might be consulted for confuting him ;
but, on the contrary, when they had got the
Trinity into his edition, threw by their manuscript, if they had one, as an almanac out of date.
And can such shuffling dealings satisfy consider-

ing men ? Let manuscripts at length be produced, and freely exposed to the sight of the learned world ; but let such manuscripts be produced as are of authority ; or else let it be confessed, that whilst Jerome pretended to correct the Latin by the Greek, the Latins have corrected both the Latin and the Greek by the sole authority of Jerome.

I. WHAT the Latins have done to this text the Greeks have done to that of St. Paul, 1 Timothy iii. 16. For by changing ὁ into ΘC, the abbreviation of Θεος, they now read, "Great is the mystery of godliness ; GOD manifested in the flesh." Whereas all the churches for the first four or five hundred years, and the authors of all the ancient versions, Jerome, as well as the rest, read, "Great is the mystery of godliness, which was manifested in the flesh." For this is the common reading of the Ethiopic, Syriac, and Latin versions to this day ; Jerome's manuscripts having given him no occasion to correct the old vulgar Latin in this place. Grotius adds the Arabic, but the Egyptian Arabic version has Θεος, and so has the above-mentioned Sclavonian version of Cyrillus ; for these two versions were made long after the sixth century, wherein the corruption began. With the ancienter versions agree the writers of the first five centuries, both Greeks and Latins. For they, in all their discourses to prove the Deity of the Son, never allege this text, that I can find, as they would all have done, and some of them frequently, had they read "God manifested in the flesh;" and therefore they read ó. Tertullian *adversus Praxeam*, and Cyprian *adversus Judæos*, industriously cite all the places where Christ is called God, but have nothing of this. Alexander of Alexandria, Athanasius, the bishops of the council of Sardica, Epiphanius, Basil, Gregory Nazianzen, Gregory Nyssen, Chrysostom, Cyril of Jerusalem, Cyril of Alexandria, Cassian, also Hilary, Lucifer, Jerome, Ambrose, Austin, Phœbadius, Victorinus Afer, Faustinus Diaconus, Pope Leo the Great, Arnobius junior, Cerealis, Vigilius Tapsensis, Fulgentius, wrote all of them in the fourth and fifth centuries, for the Deity of the Son, and incarnation of God; and some of them largely, and in several tracts; and yet I cannot find that they ever allege this text to prove it, excepting that Gregory Nyssen[1] once urges it, if the passage crept not into him out of some marginal annotation. In all the times of the hot and lasting Arian controversy, it never came into play; though, now those disputes are over, they that read "God manifested in the flesh," think it one of the most obvious and pertinent texts for the business.

[1] Orat. xi. contra Eunom.

II. The churches, therefore, of those ages were
absolute strangers to this reading. For, on the
contrary, their writers, as often as they have any
occasion to cite the reading then in use, discover
that it was ὁ. For though they cite it not to prove
the Deity of the Son, yet in their commentaries,
and sometimes in other discourses, they produce
it. And particularly Hilary (lib. 2. *de Trinitate*)
and Ambrose, or whoever of his contemporaries
was the author of the commentary on the epistles,
reads ὁ; and so doth St. Austin *in Genesin ad literam*, lib. 5: and Beda in his commentary on
this text, where he cites the reading of St. Austin,
and the author of the commentary on the epistles,
ascribed to Jerome. So also do Primasius and
Sedulius in their commentaries on this text;
and Victorinus Afer, lib. 1. *adversus Arium*; and
Idacius Clarus, or rather Vigilius Tapsensis, lib. 3.
adversus Varimadum, cap. 12; and Fulgentius,
c. 2. *de Incarnatione*; and so did Pope Leo the
Great, epist. 20. *ad Flavianum*; and Pope Gregory
the Great, lib. 34, *Moral.* cap. 7. These ancient
Latins all cite the text after this manner, " Great
is the mystery of godliness, which was manifested
in the flesh;" as the Latin manuscripts of St. Paul's
epistles generally have it to this day; and therefore it cannot be doubted, but that this hath been
the constant public reading of the Latin churches
from the beginning. So also one of the Arians
in a homily, printed in Fulgentius's works, reads
ὁ, and interprets it of the Son of God, who was

born of the Father *ante secula* ; and of the Virgin,
in novissimo tempore. And Fulgentius, in his answer to this homily, found no fault with the citation ; but, on the contrary, in his first book *ad
Trasimundum,* cap. 6, seems to have read and understood the text after the same manner with
other Latins.

III. Now for the Greeks : I find indeed that
they have changed the ancient reading of the text,
not only in the manuscripts of St Paul's epistles,
but also in other authors ; and yet there are still
remaining sufficient instances among them of
what the reading was at first. So in Chrysostom's
commentary on this epistle, they have now gotten
Θεος into the text; and yet by considering the
commentary itself, I am satisfied that he read ὁ.
For he neither in this commentary, nor anywhere
else, infers the Deity of Christ from this text ;
nor expounds it as they do who read Θεος* ; but,

---

* Nor expounds it as they do who read Θεος.] *They who
read Θεος cannot expound the passage otherwise than Chrysostom
expounds it. His words, " For God was made Man, and Man
God," are not particularly expositive of ὁ, as our author ima-
gines, but declarative of the mystery which the apostle calls the
great mystery of godliness, and they will not decide for either
reading. " Observe," says Chrysostom, " how the apostle calls
the dispensation for our sakes [the scheme of redemption] a mystery in all its branches. With good reason. For it is not known
to all men. Nay, rather it was [formerly] not known to angels.
How should it? since it has been discovered through the church.
Therefore, he says, without controversy it is great. And great
indeed it is. For God has been made Man, and Man God. A*

with the Latins, who read ὁ, understands by it
Christ incarnate ; or, as he expresses it, " Man
made God and God made man;" and so leaves it
at liberty to be taken for either God or man.
And accordingly in one place of his commentary
he saith, " Εφανερωθη εν σαρκι ὁ δημιουργος*."
In another place ; " Ανθρωπος ωφθη αναμαρτητος, ανθρωπος αναληφθη, εκηρυχθη εν κοσμῳ, μεθ᾽
ἡμων ειδον αυτον οἱ αγγελοι." " Man appeared
without sin ; Man was received up ; Man was
preached in the world ; was seen amongst us by
angels." Instead of "ὁ εφανερωθη εν σαρκι, εδικαιωθη εν πνευματι," &c. he saith, " Man appeared without sin ;" making Man the nominative case
to these, and all the verbs which follow ; which
certainly he would not have done, had Θεος been
their nominative case expressly in the text. He

---

*Man was seen without sin. A Man has been received up—
preached in the world—angels saw him with us — truly this is mystery." The design of this paraphrase of St. Chrysostom's is to
show that the scheme of redemption involves mystery in every
distinct branch mentioned by the apostle ; and our author's conclusion, that the subject of the verb εΦανερωθη, in Chrysostom's
Bible was something that might be taken either for God or man,
is at best precarious. The more natural conclusion would be, that
the common subject of the verbs εΦανερωθη, εδικαιωθη, ωΦθη, εκηρυχθη, &c. was some word that might denote a living person ; and
is not likely to have been the neuter relative ὁ.—Bp. Horsley.*

*Chrysostom's words are—λεγων, " Θεος εΦανερωθη εν σαρ-
κι," τουτεςιν, ὁ δημιουργος. Substitute ὁ for Θεος in the text
of Chrysostom, and the exposition τουτ᾽ ες ιν ὁ δημιουργος, will
be rank nonsense.—Bp. Horsley.*

might properly put man for ὁ, but not for Θεος. Neither could he have put αναμαρτητος for εδικαιωθη, if he had read in his text Θεος εδικαιωθη. For what man of common sense would say, that God was made sinless in and through the spirit? But what I have said of Chrysostom will be more evident, when I shall have shown you how afterwards, in the time of the Nestorian controversy, all parties read ὁ or ὁς, without any dispute raised about the reading; and how the Greeks have since corrupted the text in Cyril's writings, and changed ὁ and ὁς into Θεος, as they have done in Chrysostom's.

IV. And, first, that the Nestorians read ὁ is evident by some fragments of the orations or homilies of Nestorius, sent by him to the Pope, and cited by Arnobius junior, in the second book of his conflict with Serapion. For there, in order to show what was the opinion of Nestorius, and how he defended it, he cites two of his orations in these words; " *Non peperit sanctissima Maria Deitatem; nam quod natum est de carne, caro est. Non peperit creatura Creatorem; sed peperit hominem Deitatis ministrum. Non ædificavit Deum verbum Spiritus Sanctus: quod ex ipsâ natum est, de Spiritu Sancto est. Deo itaque virgo templum ex virgine ædificavit.*" Et paulo post; " *Qui per se natus est Deus in utero (scilicet ante Luciphorum) Deus est.*" Et paulo post; " Θεοτοκου *formam in Deo honoramus.*" Et in aliâ prædicatione; " *Spiritum divina separat natura, qui humanitatem ejus creavit. Quicquid ex Mariâ natum est, de Spiritu Sancto est, qui et secundum justitiam replevit, qÙod creatum est : hoc quod manifestum est in carne, justificatum est in Spiritu.*" Which last words in the language wherein Nestorius wrote those homilies, are, "ὁ εφανερωθη εν σαρκι, εδικαιωθη εν πνευματι."

V. Here you see that Nestorius reads ὁ expressly : not only so, but absolutely excludes God from being understood by it ; arguing, that the Virgin was not θεοτοκος, because that thing which was manifested in the flesh, was justified in the spirit; or, as he expounds it, replenished by the spirit in righteousness, and calling that thing which was manifested in the flesh, a creature ; " *Spiritus*," saith he, " *secundum justitiam replevit* [*hoc*] *quod creatum est* ; [*nempe*] *hoc quod manifestum est in carne, justificatum est in Spiritu.*"

VI. And now, whilst he read the text after this manner, and urged it thus against the Deity of Christ, one would suspect, that if this had not been the received public reading in the Greek churches, his adversaries would have fallen foul upon him, and exclaimed against him for falsifying the text, and blasphemously saying it was a created thing, which the Scripture calls " God manifested in the flesh." And such an accusation as this would surely have made as great a noise as anything else in the controversy ; and yet I meet with nothing of this kind in history.

His adversaries do not so much as tell him that Θεος was in the text. They were so far from raising any controversy about the reading, that they do not in the least correct him for it; but on the contrary, they themselves, in their answers to his writings, read ὁ as he did; and only laboured by various disputations to put another sense upon the text, as I find by Cassian and Cyril, the two principal who at that time wrote against him.

VII. John Cassian was Chrysostom's scholar, and his deacon and legate to the Pope; and after the banishment of Chrysostom, retired from Constantinople into Syria and Egypt, where he lived a monkish life for some time, and then ended his days in France. At that time, therefore, when Nestorius, who was patriarch of Constantinople, broached his opinion, and Cyril, the patriarch of Alexandria, opposed him; Nestorius sent a legacy to Rome with copies of his orations, to let the Pope understand the controversy: and thereupon Leo the Great, who was then archdeacon of the Church of Rome, and afterwards Pope, put Cassian (then in France) upon writing this book, *De Incarnatione Domini*, against Nestorius. He wrote it therefore in the year 430, as Baronius also reckons. For he wrote it before the condemnation of Nestorius in the council of Ephesus, as appears by the book itself. This book is now extant only in Latin; but, considering that his design in writing was to stir up the

Greek church against Nestorius, and that for the
making great impression upon them, he quotes
Greek fathers at the end of his book, and concludes with an exhortation to the citizens of Constantinople, telling them, that what he wrote for,
he had received from his master Chrysostom ; I
am satisfied that he wrote it originally in Greek:
his other books were in both languages. For
Photius saw them in eloquent Greek ; and it is
more likely that they had their author's eloquent
language from their author, and the Latin from
one of the Latins where he lived, than that the
contrary should be true. Now in this treatise[1],
when he comes to consider the passage of Nestorius about this text, of which we gave you an
account above out of Arnobius, he returns this
answer to it ; " *Jam primum enim hoc ais, Nes-
tori, quia justitiâ repleverit, quod creatum est ;
et hoc apostolico vis testimonio comprobare, quod
dicat,* apparuit in carne; justificatus est in
Spiritu ; *utrumque falso sensu et furioso spiritu
loqueris. Quia et hoc, quod à Spiritu vis eum
repletum esse justitiâ, ideo ponis, ut ostendas ejus
vacuitatem, cui præstitam esse asseras justitiæ
adimpletionem. Et hoc, quod super hâc re apostolico testimonio uteris, divini testimonii ordinem
rationemque furaris. Non enim ita ab apostolo
positum est, ut tu id truncatum vitiatumque po-
suisti. Quid enim apostolus ait?* 'Et manifestè
magnum est pietatis sacramentum, quod manifes-

---

[1] Libro septimo, cap. 18.

tum est in carne, justificatum est in Spiritu.'
Vides ergo, quod mysterium pietatis, vel sacra-
mentum justificatum apostolus prædicavit." Thus
far Cassian not only reading ὁ, but confuting
Nestorius by that reading. For whereas Nestorius said it was a creature which was justified,
Cassian tells him, that if he had read the whole
text, he would have found that it was " the
mystery of godliness." " *Vides ergo,*" saith he,
" *quod mysterium pietatis justificatum apostolus*
prædicavit." He does not say, " *Deum justifi-*
catum apostolus prædicavit " (as he would certainly have done, had that been in his Bible), but
mysterium ; and so makes *mysterium,* or, which
is all one, its relative *quod,* the nominative case
to the verbs which follow. In another part of
this treatise, lib. 5, cap. 12, Cassian cites and
interprets the text as follows ; " *Et manifestè*
magnum est pietatis sacramentum, quod manifes-
tatum est in carne, &c. Quod ergo magnum est
illud sacramentum, quod manifestatum est in carne?
Deus scilicet natus in carne, Deus visus in corpore,
qui utique sicut palam est assumptus in gloriâ."
So you see Nestorius and Cassian agree in reading ὁ, but differ in interpreting it; the one restraining it to a creature, by reason of its being
justified; the other restraining it to God, by
reason of its being a great mystery, and assumed
in glory.

VIII. In like manner, Cyril, the grand adver-
sary of Nestorius, in his three books *De Fide ad*

Imperatorem et Reginas, written against him in the beginning of that controversy, did not repre hend him, as if he had cited the text falsely, but only complained of his misinterpreting it; telling him, that he did not understand the great mystery of godliness, and that it was not a created thing, as he thought, but the Word or Son of God; and arguing for this interpretation from the circumstances of the text. And, first, in his book *De Fide ad Imperatorem,* sect. 7, he has this passage; " Πλανασθε, μη ειδοτες τας γραφας· μητε μεν το μεγα της ευσεβειας μυστηριον, τουτεστι Χρι-στον, ὁς εφανερωθη εν σαρκι, εδικαιωθη εν πνευμα-τι," &c. "Ye err," saith he, "not knowing the Scriptures, nor the great mystery of godliness, that is Christ; who was manifested in the flesh, justified in the spirit." By this citation it is plain that he read ὁς, using one of these manuscripts which, by understanding Χριστον for μυστηριον, turned ὁ into ὁς; and, by way of interpretation, inserting τουτεστι Χριστον, which in those manu-scripts was to be understood; unless you will say that he turns Θεος into ὁς, which is very hard. For had Θεος been in this text, he would not have said μυστηριον, τουτεστι Χριστον, ὁς εφανερωθη; but μυστηριον, Θεος, τουτεστι Χριστος, εφανερωθη, put-ting Χριστος, not for μυστηριον, but for Θεος. For Χριστος and Θεος are more plainly equipollent than Χριστος and μυστηριον. And making Χριστος and μυστηριον equipollent, he makes μυστηριον the nomi-native case to εφανερωθη; and therefore read them

joined in this text by the article ὁς. Had he read
Θεος, he would never have left out that authentic
and demonstrative word, and by way of interpretation for μυςηριον Θεος written Χριςον ὁς. For
this was not to argue against Nestorius, but to
spoil the argument which lay before him. Neither
would he have gone on, as he does, within a few
lines, to recite the same text, putting λογος by way
of interpretation for μυςηριον; and after to pro-
pound it as his bare opinion, that the Word or
Son of God was here to be understood by this mystery, and to dispute for this his opinion, as
needing proof out of other texts of Scripture, as
he does after this manner[1] : " Moreover," saith
he, " in my opinion, that mystery of godliness
is nothing else than he who came to us from
God the Father; the Word, who was manifested in the flesh. For in taking the form of
a servant, he was born of the holy God-bearing
Virgin," &c. And then, after many other things,
he at length in sect. 23 and 24, concludes, that
" this divine mystery is above our understanding ;
and that the only-begotten, who is God, and, according to the Scriptures, the Lord of all things,
appeared to us, was seen on earth, and became
man." This he makes not the text itself, but the
interpretation thereof; and from the preceding disputation, concludes it to be genuine.

[1] " Ειη γαρ αν ουχ ἱτερον οιμαι τι το της ευσεβειας μυστηριον,
η αυτος ἡμιν ὁ εκ Θεου πατρος λογος, ὁς εφανερωθη εν σαρκι.
Γεγενηται γαρ δια της ἁγιας παρθινου και θεοτοκου, μορφην
δουλον λαβων." Cyril. de Fide ad Imperatorem, Sect. 8.

IX. Again, in the first of his two treatises, *De Fide ad Reginas,* near the end, he cites the text, and argues thus against the interpretation of Nestorius. " Who is he," saith he, " that is manifested in the flesh ?   Is it not fully evident, that it is no other than the Word of God the Father ? For so will that be a great mystery of godliness (which was [1] manifested in the flesh) ; he was seen of angels, ascending into heaven ; he was preached to the Gentiles by the holy apostles ; he was believed on in the world, but this not as a mere man ; but as God born in the flesh, and after our manner."

X. So also in his second book, *De fide ad Reginas* [2], he cites the place again ; and then argues upon it against the opinion of Nestorius after this manner : " If the Word, being God, is said to become a man, and yet continue what he was before, without losing his Deity, the mystery of godliness is without doubt a very great one ; but if Christ be a mere man, joined with God only in the parity of dignity and power (for this is maintained by some unlearned men), how is he manifested in the flesh ?   Is it not plain, that every man is in the flesh, and cannot otherwise be seen by any body ? how then was he said to be seen of the holy angels ? For do they not also see us ? What was there therefore new or extraordinary in Christ, if the angels saw him such a man as we are, and

---

[1] Codex Græcus hoc loco jam legit ΘC pro ὅς sensu perturbato.   [2] Sect. 33.

nothing more," &c. Thus Cyril goes on to give his reasons why that which was manifested in the flesh, was not a mere created Man, as Nestorius interpreted, but the eternal Word, or Son of God; all which would have been very superfluous and impertinent, if *God* had then been expressly in the text.

XI. Seeing therefore Nestorius alleged the text to prove, that it was a created thing which was manifested in the flesh; and Cyril, in confuting him, did not answer that it was *God* expressly in the text, nor raise any debate about the reading, qut only put another interpretation upon the text than Nestorius had done; arguing with Cassian, that in the text it was not a mere man, as Nestorius contended, but a great mystery of godliness; and by consequence Christ, or God the Son, which was manifested in the flesh; and labouring by divers other arguments to prove this interpretation; it is evident beyond all cavil, that Cyril was a stranger to Θεος, now got into the text; and read ὁς or ὁ, as Nestorius and Cassian did.

XII. And all this is further confirmed by Photius, who, in his commentary on the epistles not yet published, relates that Cyril, in the 12th chapter of his Scholiums, read "ὁς εφανερωθη," &c.; and consonant to this reading is Cyril's commentary upon the text in his explanation of the second of the twelve Anathematisms, where he puts the question, "*Quid est igitur quod dicit, apparuit in carne?*" And explains it by saying, "*Hoc est,*

Dei patris verbum caro factum est;" and concludes, that it is hence that we call him God and Man. Whereas had Θεος been in the text, it would have needed no interpretation; nor would he have put λογος for Θεος, in order to prove that God was manifested in the flesh. And yet in his books *ad Reginas*, and his other writings, wherever he quotes this text, the Greeks have since corrected it by their corrected manuscripts of St. Paul's epistles, and written Θεος instead of ὁ; whence, if you would truly understand the Nestorian history, you must read ὁ or ὁς for Θεος in all Cyril's citations of this text.

XIII. Now, whilst Cyril read ὁ or ὁς, and in the explanation of the twelve chapters, or articles, quoted this text in the second article; and this explanation was recited by him in the council of Ephesus, and approved by the council[1], with an anathema at the end of every article; it is manifest that this council allowed the reading ὁς or ὁ; and by consequence that ὁς or ὁ was the authentic, public, uncontroverted reading till after the times of this council. For if Nestorius and Cyril, the patriarchs of Constantinople and Alexandria, and the heads of the two parties in this controversy, read ὁς or ὁ; and their writings went about amongst the Eastern churches, and were canvassed by the bishops and clergy without any dispute raised about the reading; and if Cyril read ὁς by the approbation of the council itself;

[1] Concil. Ephes. par. iii. sub initio.

I think that the conclusion we make of its being then the general uncontroverted reading must
needs be granted us.   And if the authority of one
of the four first general councils make anything
for the truth of the reading, we have that into the
bargain.

XIV. Yet whilst the Nestorian controversy
brought the text into play, and the two parties
ran the interpretation into extremes, the one disputing that ὁ or ὁς was a creature, the other that
it was the Word of God ; the prevalence of the
latter party made it pass for the orthodox opinion,
that ὁ or ὁς was God ; and so gave occasion to
the Greeks henceforward to change the language
of *Christ* into that of *God*; and say, in their ex-
positions of the text, that God was manifested in
the flesh (as I find Theodoret doth), and at length
to write *God* in the text itself; the easy change
of O or OC into ΘC, inviting them to do it; and,
if this was become the orthodox authentic reading, to set right the text in Chrysostom, Cyril,
Theodoret, and wherever else they found it (in
their opinion), corrupted by heretics.

XV. And the man that first began thus to alter
the sacred text, was Macedonius, the patriarch of
Constantinople, in the beginning of the sixth
century ; for the Emperor Anastasius banished
him for corrupting it.   At that time the Greek
church had been long divided about the council
of Chalcedon.   Many who allowed the condemnation of Eutyches, rejected the council ; by

E

r
eason of its decreeing, by the influence of the
bishop of Rome's letter against Eutyches, that
Christ subsisted not only *ex duabus naturis,* which
Eutyches allowed, but also *in duabus naturis;*
which language was new to the Greeks, and by a
great part of that church taken for Nestorianism.
For they understood, that as the body and soul
made the nature of Man, so God and Man made
the nature of Christ ; assigning the nature to the
person of Christ, as well as to all other things,
and not considering that in all compounds the
several parts have also their several natures.
Hence each party endeavoured to render the other
suspected of heresy ; as if they that were for the
council secretly favoured the Nestorians, and they
that were against it the Eutychians. For one
part, in maintaining two distinct natures in Christ,
were thought to deny the nature of one person
with Nestorius ; and the other party, in opposing
two distinct natures in him, were thought to deny
the truth of one of the natures with Eutyches.
Both parties, therefore, to clear themselves of
those imputations, anathematized both those he-
resies ; and therefore, whilst they thus differed in
their modes of speaking, they agreed in their
sense, as Evagrius well observes. But the bishops
of Rome and Alexandria being engaged against
one another, and for a long time distracting the
East by these disputes ; at length the Emperor
Zeno, to quiet his empire, and perhaps to secure it
from the encroachment of the bishop of Rome, who,

by this verbal contest[1], aspired to the name and authority of universal bishop, sent about an *henoticum*, or pacificatory decree ; wherein he anathematized both Nestorius and Eutyches with their followers on the one hand, and abrogated the Pope's letter and the council on the other; and his successor, Anastasius, for the same end, laboured for to have this decree signed by all the bishops. And Macedonius at first subscribed it ; but afterwards heading those who stood up for the council[2], was, for corrupting the Scriptures in favour of his opinion, and such other things as were laid to his charge, deposed and banished, ann. C. 512[3]. But his own party, which at length prevailed, defended him, as if oppressed by calumnies ; and so received that reading for genuine, which he had put about among them. For how ready are all parties to receive what they reckon on their side, Jerome well knew, when he recommended the testimony of " the Three in Heaven" by its usefulness ; and we have a notable instance of it in the last age, when the churches, both Eastern and Western, received this testimony in a moment in their Greek Testaments, and still continue with great zeal and pas-

[1] Vide Baronium, anno 451 ; sect. 149, 150, 151.

[2] Evagrius, lib. iii. cap. xxi. 44.—Theodorus lector, lib. ii. and Marcellini Chronicon.

[3] Flavian was banished in the year of Antioch 561, as Evagrius notes ; and Macedonius was banished the same year, or the year before

sion to defend it for the ancient reading, against the authority of all the Greek manuscripts.

XVI. But now I have told you the original of the corruption, I must tell you my author; and he is Liberatus, archdeacon of the church of Carthage, who lived in that very age. For in his Breviary, which he wrote in the year 535, or soon after, and collected, as he saith in his preface, out of Greek records, he delivers it in these words[1]:

" *Hoc tempore Macedonius Constantinopolitanus episcopus ab imperatore Anastasio dicitur expulsus, tanquam evangelia falsaret ; et maxime illud apostoli dictum,* Quia apparuit in carne, justificatum in spiritu. *Hunc enim mutasse, ubi habet* qui .... *hoc est* .... *monosyllabum Græcum, literâ mutatâ in* .... *vertisse et fecisse* .... *id est, ut esset Deus, apparuit per carnem. Tanquam Nestorianus ergo culpatus expellitur per severum Monachum*[2]." The Greek letters here omitted are, in the second edition of Sunius, and in those of the councils, thus inserted : " *Ubi habet* ὁς, *hoc est* qui, *monosyllabum Græcum, literâ mutatâ o in* ω, *vertisse et fecisse* ὡς ; *id est, ut esset, Deus apparuit per carnem.*" But this interpolation was surely made by conjecture ; for if Θεος was in the sacred text before the corruption, then ὁς or ὁ was not in, and so could not be changed into ὡς : but if Θεος was not in, it could not be brought in by this change. The interpolation therefore is in-

[1] Liberati Brev. cap. xix.
[2] Vide Baronii Annal. 510. sect. 9.

consistent and spurious, and seems to have been occasioned by straining to make out Nestorianism here; the scribes, for that end[1], referring the words *ut esset* to the sacred text; and then the interpolator writing ὡς for *ut*. Whereas they should have referred *ut esset* to the words of Liberatus, thus distinguished from the sacred text; " *Id est, ut esset,* Deus apparuit per carnem." I had rather, therefore, waive the conjecture of this interpolator, and fill up the *lacunæ* by the authority of an ancient author, Hincmarus; who above eight hundred years ago[2] related the fact out of Liberatus after this manner: " *Quidam ipsas Scripturas verbis illicitis imposturaverunt ; sicut Macedonius Constantinopolitanus episcopus, qui ab Anastasio Imperatore ideo a civitate expulsus legitur, quoniam falsavit evangelia; et illum apostoli locum, quod apparuit in carne, justificatum est in spiritu; per cognationem Græcarum literarum* O *et* Θ *hoc modo mutando falsavit. Ubi enim habuit,* qui, *hoc est* OC, *monosyllabum Græcum, literâ mutatâ* O *in* Θ, *mutavit, et fecit* ΘC, *id est, ut esset, Deus apparuit per carnem; quapropter tanquam Nestori-*

---

[1] N.B. In Hincmari opusc. xxxiii. cap. 22. the words *ut esset* are in like manner referred to the sacred text; and somebody, to make out the sense, has in their stead added *ut appareret* to the words of Liberatus, and written *ut appareret, ut esset Deus,* &c. But the words *ut appareret* not being in Liberatus, must be struck out, and supplied by setting the comma after *ut esset,* to part these words from the sacred text.

[2] Hincmari opusc. artic. xxxiii. cap. 18.

unus fuit expulsus." He was banished therefore
for changing the ancient reading (which in some
manuscripts was OC, as these authors have it, and
in others O) into ΘC. But whereas he is here represented a Nestorian for doing this, the meaning
is, that he was banished for corrupting the text in
favour of the doctrine of two natures in Christ ;
which his enemies accounted Nestorianism, though
it was not really so. Nestorius held only a human
nature in Christ ; and that God, *the Word,* dwelt
in this nature, as the spirit in a holy man; and
therefore interpreted ò of the human nature. This
doctrine Macedonius anathematized, and maintained two natures in Christ ; and, for proving
this, corrupted the text, and made it *God manifested in the flesh.* This distinguishing Christ
into two natures was, by the enemies of Macedonius, accounted Nestorianism in another language ; and in this respect the historian saith, that
they banished him as a Nestorian for corrupting
the text, though he was not really of that opinion.

XVII. But whilst he is said to be banished as
a Nestorian for this, without explaining what is
here meant by a Nestorian, it looks like a trickish way of speaking, used by his friends to ridicule the proceedings against him as inconsistent ;
perhaps to invert the crime of falsation ; as if a
Nestorian would rather change ΘC into O. For
they that read history with judgement, will too
often meet with such trickish reports ; and even
in the very story of Macedonius I meet with some

other reports of the same kind. For Macedonius having in his keeping the original acts of the council of Chalcedon, signed by that emperor under whom it was called, and refusing to deliver up this book to the emperor Anastasius; some, to make this emperor perjured, distorted the story; as if, at his coming to the crown, he had promised under his hand and oath, that he would not act against the council of Chalcedon; and represented his subscribed promise to be the book, which Macedonius refused to deliver back to him. Macedonius had got his bishopric by being against the council of Chalcedon, and had subscribed the *henoticum*[1] of Zeno, in which that council was anathematized; and this being objected against him, his friends, to stifle the accusation, make a contrary story of the emperor; as if, when he came to the crown, he had done as much as that in behalf of the council. Another report was[2], "That the people of Alexandria and all Egypt, great and small, bond and free, priests and monks, excepting only strangers, became about this time possessed with evil spirits, and being deprived of human speech, barked day and night like dogs; so that they were afterwards bound with iron chains, and drawn to the church, that they might recover their health. For they all ate their hands and arms. And then an angel appeared to some of the people, saying, that this happened to them

[1] Vide Annotationes Valesii in Evagr. &c. lib. iii. cap. 31.
[2] Victor Turonensis in Chronico.

because they anathematized the council of Chalcedon, and threatened that they should do so no more." Again, we are told in history[1], " That the adversaries of Macedonius produced certain boys in judgement to accuse both him and themselves of sodomy; but that when they found his genitals were cut off, they betook themselves to other arts for deposing him." Now if you can believe that a eunuch had the beard and voice of another man; and that in a solemn council the great patriarch of the East was thus accused and thus acquitted, and yet deposed; you must acknowledge that there were many bishops among the Greeks who would not stick at as ill and shameless things as corrupting the Scriptures. But if all this be a sham invented to discredit the council, the need of such shams adds credit to their proceedings in condemning him for a falsary.

XVIII. This council, if I mistake not, sat first at Constantinople, being that council which Theodorus calls "a company of mercenary wretches;" and Nicephorus, " a convention of heretics, assembled against Macedonius." Upon their adding to the " thrice holy" these words[2], " who art crucified for us," the people fell into a tumult; and afterwards, when Macedonius came to be accused, they fell into a greater tumult, crying out, " The time of persecution is at hand; let no man

---

[1] Evagrius, lib. iii. cap. 32.
[2] Theodor. lib. ii.—Nicephor. lib. xvi. cap. 26.—Evagr. lib. iii. cap. 44.

desert the father ;" meaning Macedonius. In this tumult, which was said to be stirred up by the clergy of Constantinople, many parts of the city were burnt, and the nobles and emperor brought into the greatest danger ; insomuch that the emperor was forced to proffer the resignation of his empire, before he could quiet the multitude. Then seeing that, if Macedonius were judged, the people would defend him, he caused him to be carried by force in the night to Chalcedon ; and thence into banishment, as Theodorus writes. Whence I gather, that the council removed also to Chalcedon to avoid the tumult, and finish their proceeding there. For the story of his being accused in judgement by boys, Nicephorus places after this tumult; and all agree that he was condemned ; and the monks of Palestine, in an epistle recorded by Evagrius, say that Xenaias and Dioscorus, joined with many bishops, banished him. When his condemnation was sent him, signed by the emperor, he asked, whether they that had condemned him received the council of Chalcedon ; and when they that brought him the sentence denied it, he replied, " If Arians and Macedonians had sent me a book of condemnation, could I receive it ?" So that it seems he stood upon the illegality of the council. The next day one Timothy was made bishop of Constantinople, and he sent about the condemnation of Macedonius to all the absent bishops to be subscribed [1].

[1] Theophanes, p. 135.

Whence I think it will easily be granted, that he was condemned as a falsary by the greatest part of the Eastern empire ; and by consequence, that the genuine reading was till then, by the churches of that empire, accounted ὀ. For had not the public reading then been ὀ, there could have been no colour for pretending that he changed it into ΘC.

XIX. About six years after Anastasius died, and his successors, Justin and Justinian, set up the authority of the council of Chalcedon again, together with that of the Pope over the Eastern churches, as universal bishop ; and from that time the friends of Macedonius prevailing, it is probable, that in opposition to the heretics, which condemned him, and for promoting and establishing the doctrine of two natures in Christ, they received and spread abroad the reading ΘC. But as for the authority of the Pope, that fell again with Rome in the Gothic wars, and slept till Phocas revived it.

XX. I told you of several shams put about by the friends of Macedonius, to discredit the proceedings of the council against him. There is one which notably confirms what has hitherto been said, and makes it plain that his friends received his corruptions as genuine Scripture. For whereas Macedonius was banished for corrupting the New Testament, his friends retorted the crime upon the council, as if they had taken upon them, under colour of purging the Scriptures from the corruptions of Macedonius, to correct in them whatever they thought the Apostles, as unskilful men and idiots, had written amiss. For this I gather from an ironical report of this kind put about in the West, and thus recorded by Victor Turonensis: *" Messald V. C. consulibus, Constantinopoli, jubente Anastasio Imperatore, sancta evangelia, tanquam ab idiotis composita, reprehenduntur et emendantur;"* that is, " In the consulship of Messala, the holy gospels, by the command of the emperor Anastasius, were censured and corrected at Constantinople, as if written by evangelists that were idiots." Here Victor errs in the year. For Messala was consul anno Christi 506, that is, six years before the banishment of Macedonius. But Victor is very uncertain in dates of the years; for he places the banishment of Macedonius in the consulship of Avienus 502; and the above-mentioned tumult about the *Trisagium* in the consulship of Probus, anno Christi 513; whereas all these things happened in the same year. For it is plain by this chronicle, that the Scriptures were examined and corrected about this time by a council at Constantinople, by the order of Anastasius ; and I meet with no other council to which this character can agree, besides that which deposed Macedonius. Now that they should censure and correct the gospels, as if written by idiots, is too plainly ironical to be true history ; and therefore it must be an abusive report, invented and put about to ridicule and shame the council, and to propagate the corruptions of Macedonius as the genuine apostolic reading of the Scriptures, which the council had rashly corrected.

XXI. So then the falsation was set on foot in the beginning of the fifth century, and is now of about twelve hundred years standing ; and therefore since it lay but in a letter, and so was more easily spread abroad in the Greek manuscripts than the testimony of " the Three in Heaven" in the Latin ones, we need not wonder if the old reading be scarce to be met with in any Greek manuscripts now extant ; and yet it is in some.

XXII. For though Beza tells us that all the Greek manuscripts read Θεoc, yet I must tell Beza's readers, that all his manuscripts read ὁ. For he had no other manuscripts of the epistles besides the Claromontan ; and in this manuscript, as Morinus by ocular inspection has since informed us, the ancient reading was ὁ[1] : but yet in another hand, and with other ink, the letter Θ has been written out of the line ; and the letter O, thickened to make a C, appears ; which instance shows sufficiently by whom the ancient reading has been

---

[1] Aliâ manu et atramento, extra lineæ seriem, addita est litera Θ, et ambesa paululum O, ut appareret sigma. Sed præpostera emendatio facile conspicitur. *Hæc Morinus in Exercitationibus Biblicis, lib.* i. *Exercitat.* ii. *cap.* 4.—At Beza nobis aliqua invidit, ut ex ejus epistolâ ad Academiam Cantabrigiensem a Waltono editâ, liquet ; ubi variantes aliquas lectiones celandas esse admonet.

changed. Valesius also read ὁ in one of the Spanish manuscripts ; and so did the author of the
Oxford edition of the New Testament, ann. Ch.
1675, in the manuscript of Lincoln College library,
which is the oldest of the Oxford manuscripts.
The Alexandrian manuscript[1] and one of Colbert's,
and Cyril, c. 12. Scholiorum (teste Photio MS.
com. in Epist.), read OC. So then there are
some ancient Greek manuscripts which read ὁ,
and others ὁς ; but I do not hear of any Latin
ones, either ancient or modern, which read Θεος.

XXIII. And besides to read Θεος makes the
sense obscure and difficult. For how can it properly be said, "that God was justified in the spi-

---

[e] Alio atramento jam ducta cernitur tam lineola per medium
literæ O, quam virgula superna ; ut jam legatur ΘC. Putat
autem Millius, lineolas illas olim tenues fuisse et prope evani-
das, et novo dein atramento incrassatas fuisse ; eo quod per-
lustrato attentius loco, lineolæ per medium Θ ductæ, quæ
primam aciem fugerat, ductus quosdam ac vestigia satis certa
deprehendere visus esset ; præsertim ad partem sinistram, quæ
peripheriam literæ pertingit ; luculentiora multo habiturus
nisi obstante liturâ quam dixit hodiernâ lineolæ ipsi superin-
ductâ. Verum si lineola antiquitus tam conspicua esset, ut
usque nunc per medium lineæ crassioris, alio atramento superinductæ, cerni possit ; quid opus esset, ut a lineâ illâ superin-
ductâ incrassaretur ? Sin olim tam evanida esset, ut cerni vix
posset ; mirum est, quod ejus ductus et vestigia satis certa,
per medium literæ illius superinductæ, etiamnum appareant.
Doceant verba evanida aliis in locis atramento novo incrassata
fuisse, vel fateantur OC hic mutatum in ΘC.

rit ?"* But to read ὁ, and interpret it of Christ, as the ancient Christians did, without restraining it to his divinity, makes the sense very easy. For the promised and long-expected Messias, the hope of Israel, is to us "the great mystery of godliness." And this mystery was at length manifested to the Jews from the time of his baptism, and justified to be the person whom they expected.

XXIV. I have now given you an account of the corruption of the text, the sum of which is this; the difference between the Greek and the ancient versions puts it past dispute, that either the Greeks have corrupted their manuscripts, or the Latins, Syrians, and Ethiopians their versions; and it is more reasonable to lay the fault upon the Greeks than upon the other three, for these considerations. It was easier for one nation to do it than for three to conspire. It was easier to change a letter or two in the Greek, than six words in the Latin. In the Greek, the sense is obscure; in the versions, clear. It was agreeable to the interest of the Greeks to make the change,

* *How is it said in St. Luke, that "publicans justified God" by receiving John's baptism? If to read Θεος gives a difficult sense in this clause, to read ὁ, will it give an easy sense in others? Are the propositions, that a mystery was manifested in the flesh, a mystery was received up into glory, both which arise from the reading ὁ, very easily intelligible? Is it easy to understand what mystery was manifested in the flesh, if our Lord's divinity is set out of the question? If it be allowed that his divinity makes the mystery, the two readings will be equivalent in sense, but Θεος makes the best construction.*—Bp. Horsley.

but against the interest of other nations to do it; and men are never false to their interest. The Greek reading was unknown in the times of the Arian controversy; but that of the versions then in use amongst both Greeks and Latins. Some Greek manuscripts render the Greek reading dubious; but those of the versions hitherto collated agree. There are no signs of corruption in the versions hitherto discovered; but in the Greek we have showed you particularly when, on what occasion, and by whom, the text was corrupted.

XXV. I know not whether it be worth the while to tell you, that in the printed works of Athanasius, there is an epistle *De incarnatione verbi*, which reads Θεος. For this epistle relates to the Nestorian heresy, and so was written by a much later author than Athanasius, and may also possibly have been since corrected, like the works of Chrysostom and Cyril, by the corrected texts of St. Paul's Epistles. I have had so short a time to run my eye over authors, that I cannot tell whether, upon further search, more passages about this falsation may not hereafter occur pertinent to the argument. But if there should, I presume it will not be difficult, now the falsation is thus far laid open, to know what construction to put upon them, and how to apply them.

XXVI. You see what freedom I have used in this discourse, and I hope you will interpret it candidly. For if the ancient churches, in debating and deciding the greatest mysteries of religion, knew nothing of these two texts, I understand not, why we should be so fond of them now the debates are over. And whilst it is the character of an honest man to be pleased, and of a man of interest to be troubled at the detection of frauds, and of both to run most into those passions when the detection is made plainest ; I hope this letter will, to one of your integrity, prove so much the more acceptable, as it makes a further discovery than you have hitherto met with in commentators.

THE END.

Milton Keynes UK
Ingram Content Group UK Ltd.
UKHW011315301023
431603UK00001B/57